Seen and not Heard

Jennifer Jane Sherriff

ISBN: 978-1-291-59745-5

Acknowledgments

Jenny Oxley, Mill Green Museum, Hatfield for opening up the Sherriff files.

Photograph acknowledgements

Kate Jewell: for her photograph of Old Croxton Park House

David Stirling: Waltham on the Wolds local history for his panoramic view of Croxton Park

To my siblings for unwittingly being part of my story,

Front cover: Rob Sharples

CONTENTS

Introduction

I have been inspired to write this story from my memories as a child. I was born just before the so called 'baby boomers' – a generation that was supposed to have it all. But for many, it was not a life of privilege and luxury.

Life was vastly different than it is today. Traditional values were very important and strictly upheld and family matters never discussed in front of the children. This often led to years of anguish for children who did not understand family tragedies and the events surrounding them, and being too afraid to ask.

As a young girl, and then as a teenager in the 1950s and '60s, I continued to feel responsible for the sad and confusing events that took place in my own family.

I was of the era when children were seen and not heard, but by putting pen to paper as an adult helped me to make sense of a world that I did not understand as a child.

Chapter One - The Ancestors

Friday - the day of our family get-together. Already late, I was rushing out to the car, when a sudden thought occurred to me: my holiday snaps. I couldn't turn up to see my brother and sisters without my latest photographs. But where had I put them?

I rummaged frantically through the drawer, but they were nowhere to be found. Positive that I had seen them the previous week, I wrenched the drawer from the sideboard and tipped the contents onto the floor. Marbles, drawing pins and half-used candles came clattering out, but there were no photos.

A faded brown envelope was sandwiched between some pamphlets and old newspaper cuttings. Hastily I emptied the contents from the envelope, but the photographs inside weren't the ones I was expecting to see: they were of Grandfather Wilfred. I was mesmerized by the face that was looking back at me, but I couldn't dilly-dally as I had a long journey ahead.

Upon arriving at my brother's house I had to get involved with all the things families do when they haven't seen each other for a long time, but my mind kept going back to those photographs. I couldn't help wondering how long they'd been in that drawer, as I had never seen them before. Maybe some mysterious being had intended me to find them, I thought fancifully.

Returning home a few days later, I made a beeline for the old brown envelope, as I was captivated by this handsome young man and sensed an affinity and a closeness that I couldn't explain. Perhaps I'd inherited my grandfather's mischievous ways and the twinkle in his eyes…?

Coming across these photographs made me want to delve deeper into my family background and it was in Hertfordshire that my search began. I discovered that Wilfred's father, Arthur James Sherriff, left Aylesbury in 1872 with his wife Annie and young family. In so doing, he was leaving behind his forefathers' traditional role as governors of the Buckinghamshire county jail. The family moved to Hatfield, whereupon Arthur James set up his coal and corn merchant business, prior to becoming tenants of the Salisbury estate.

Wilfred was born in 1882 and being the fourth in a family of eleven siblings, the family ultimately outgrew their home in Park Street. Then in 1896 they moved to a house in Mill Green. This fine residence: known as Leaside, was built especially for Arthur James and his expanding family by the 3rd Marquess of Salisbury, who at the time was Prime Minister of the United Kingdom.

Along with this substantial place came the necessity for a cook and housemaids, and for the children – nursemaids, as it was a time when servants were part of everyday life and taken for granted by all middle-class families. It also provided much needed employment for those who were less well off.

Over the following years my great-grandfather built his fortune by way of his corn and coal enterprise. He also farmed at Cromer Hyde and Lemsford, a short distance from Mill Green. Nevertheless, with nine surviving brothers and sisters, assets were not sufficient to share amongst them all, as a result, only the first-born siblings entered into the family business.

For this reason Wilfred went into the banking profession, which was considered a respectable occupation for a well-connected young man. Then in later years he returned to farming, which had been part of his family background.

Wilfred's photographs show a dashing young man, so I'm sure he would have been popular with the ladies, but it was a young girl from another farming family who won his heart. With her golden locks and irresistible smile, Mary Ellen became Wilfred's true love. Born in 1880 at Highfield Farm, Ramsey Hollow, where her father, John Dumella Rose, and his father before him employed fifteen men and six boys to farm the five hundred acres.

When young, Mary Ellen attended Prospect House, a local boarding school for girls in St. Neots, but with few employment opportunities for educated young ladies in the area, she moved to the village of Chorlton-cum-Hardy in Lancashire, where she became a governess to a young girl, also called Mary. Mary Ellen's new home was a great distance from Huntingdon; consequently she saw little of Wilfred. Nevertheless, they continued to communicate by writing long letters, until eventually, he asked for her hand in marriage.

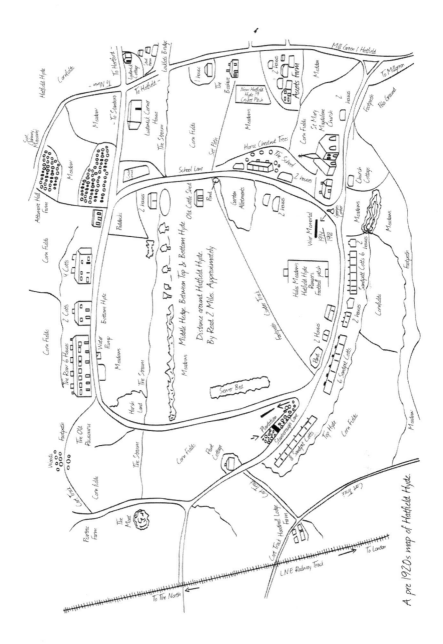

A pre 1920s map of Hatfield Hyde.

5

After their wedding in 1910, Mary Ellen and Wilfred moved to Ludwick Cottage in Hatfield Hyde. With Wilfred being in the Cavalry Division of the 13th London Regiment Royal Welsh Fusiliers, and living adjacent to Ludwick Stud Farm: which was used to train horses during the Great War, it is likely he was involved with their training before they were sent to France. On many occasions horses were to be seen around the lanes in Hatfield Hyde, drawing gun limbers as part of their training.

Mary Ellen's life was much changed after her marriage, and with maids to do the household chores; she had the time to pursue her love of needlework and picture painting - these being quintessential activities for gentlewomen in the early 20th century.

However, their stay at Ludwick Cottage was brief, as a few years later they moved to Ascots Farm, on another part of the Salisbury estate, and here the Sherriff farming tradition continued. Then aged thirty-six, Mary Ellen gave birth to her first child. Quite old for a first baby, so perhaps Wilfred's wartime duties had taken him to foreign lands. Monday 15th May 1916 was when my father, John Dumella, arrived into the world, although another four years passed before his sister, Freda, was born.

With many political, social and economic problems post-war, there was a great deal of unrest amongst the working classes. On the contrary, it was a golden age for house builders and farmers. Consequently, Wilfred's children had many opportunities associated with the wealthier classes. And also private education, though Father's fees to attend Bedford School were paid by a wealthy aunt.

Regardless of these privileges, Father seldom talked about his childhood. Maybe growing up in the Edwardian era, when a child's upbringing was disciplined and strictly controlled, had something to do with this. Not only that, a great deal of time was spent in the care of the nanny, rather than in the company of parents.

Despite Ascots Farm being a wonderful place for the children, and close to their many aunts, uncles and cousins, around the time of 1926 Wilfred and Mary Ellen moved from the area. This in all probability arose due to the acquisition of land from Lord Salisbury, when many tenanted farms on his estate were taken over to make way for the new town of Welwyn Garden City.

The change of direction took them to Little Barford in Bedfordshire. Located thirty odd miles from Hatfield, and close to the A1 Great North Road, it was ideally placed. Here my grandfather took over the tenancy of Rectory Farm, and this is where, over the following years my father went from boyhood into adulthood and then into having a family of his own.

Wilfred's new venture involved many hours of work, as a result, he saw little of his children. He made up for these absent times by taking them to London to see the West End shows and with his cousin, R. C. Sherriff, being a famous author and playwright, when his play *Journey's End* was performed at the Apollo Theatre, my father who was about twelve years of age, and his sister, went along too. After the performance, they went backstage to meet some of the artists, including the young Laurence Olivier.

The move to Rectory Farm proved very successful, with arable, dairy farming and pigs. Wilfred was carrying on this family tradition, as throughout the 1920s, and thereafter, the Sherriff's had become leading pig breeders in the country, with many of their prize winners: the Gloucester Old Spot, Berkshire and Middle Whites being exported to foreign lands.

Sadly, Wilfred's happiness was not to last, as it was in 1942 that Mary Ellen died after a tragic accident. Broken-hearted, he moved to Cambridge to start a new life. At which point, my father, who had worked on the farm since boyhood, took over the tenancy. He was young and forward thinking, a modern farmer and ahead of his times.

The Cross Family
My maternal grandparents, the Cross family, had been yeoman farmers since the 16th century, with parcels of land in the Berkshire and Buckinghamshire region. My great-grandfather, George Robert Cross, farmed at Barge Farm, Taplow, in Buckinghamshire, where he employed eleven men and four boys to work the three hundred and sixty acres. He became well-known when his chestnut gelding, Forester, won the Chertsey Steeplechase in 1863, clearing a thirty-two foot jump. A year later, another of his horses: Confederate, won at the Chertsey Steeplechase, with the winner's cup being presented by a representative of the Royal Horse Guards.

My grandfather, Arthur Cross, didn't go into farming or indeed, anything to do with horses. He went into the banking profession, and in later life, became a manager with the Westminster Bank in Biggleswade. But he still loved country life, and lawn bowls, a sport at which he became a champion many times over.

Minnie Cross, my maternal grandmother, died quite young so we never met. All I have are photographs indicating that she was a lovely lady, looking elegant and so refined. Minnie had five children, the first being my mother, Dorothy. She and her siblings were brought up at a time when good manners and graciousness were part of a child's education. But they had fun times too. Particularly, when practising for the musical shows and dancing events which they performed at family occasions.

Aunt Win, friend, Aunt Margaret and Dorothy (my mother) circa 1917

Their outfits were made especially for them by their mother or the dressmaker, as all items of clothing - daywear and nightwear, were handmade. Is this where my fantasy notions came from I wonder?

Like lots of little girls I wanted to wear pretty clothes. I also wanted to be a princess, and of course, wear a tiara. Throughout childhood, I daydreamed of this other life, which I believed was somewhere out there waiting for me. After all, I had been taught to speak nicely and had good manners. Surely I was perfect for such a role? Or in reality, was it because, as the youngest of three girls, I was always the one to get the hand-me-down clothes and merely wanted something better for my life?

Fortunately my mother, being the first born, didn't have to wear second-hand dresses. However, her destiny, as the eldest daughter, was that upon leaving school she was expected to stay at home and assist with looking after her younger siblings – and continued to do so until her brother left home to fight in the Second World War.

And even though my father was fortunate by most standards, he didn't have the same charmed life as my mother, as he had to do work on the farm throughout his childhood. Attending Bedford School as a day boy was a privilege, but not before rising early in the morning to perform tasks on the farm - such as stoking the steam ploughing engines ready for the farm labourers to carry out their duties. He may not have been top of the class, nonetheless, he went on to gain his papers to enter into the banking profession, but farming was the family tradition.

In spite of my mother being older than my father, he was captivated by her charm and gentle manner. In fact, they were a perfect match. She was tall, slim and pretty, whilst my father: like any well-bred young man, was eloquent and courteous; and very handsome too. Tennis was their passion, but they also loved musical shows and living within easy reach of London and a train journey costing 2/6d, it was easy for them to visit the West End.

Not ballet or opera though. Father loved something to get his toes tapping: dancing music. And he certainly looked the part when dressed up for an evening out, his collars and cuffs were starched to perfection, and I so loved the white silk scarf that he, and every well-dressed gentleman wore. Passionate about Johann Strauss, with the Viennese waltz his favourite dance.

Mother also loved to dance and when young, she and Aunt Win attended the local events. Winifred, being several years younger, had to be chaperoned by her sister, as young ladies weren't allowed out alone and had to be escorted by an older person. The two of them weren't just sisters, they were also best friends.

Numerous old photographs show the Cross family on holiday, Walton on Naze being a favourite place, with Grandpa Cross chauffeuring them in his beautiful black limousine. Then after a paddle in the sea, they sat outside their beach hut and sipped afternoon tea. Such an elegant lifestyle and all in a bygone era.

Rectory Farm

After Mary Ellen's death, my parents took over the running of Rectory Farm. The twins, Robert and MaryAnn, were almost two years old when they were joined by a new baby - Angela. Then I was born fourteen months later in Huntingdon General Hospital; it was Friday the 25th August 1944 and the day that Paris was liberated from the Germans in the Second World War. Not knowing whether I was going to be a boy or girl, my parents had not chosen a name. What's more, I remained nameless for many weeks, until eventually, they came up with Jennifer Jane.

Tempsford Air Disaster

Shortly after my arrival into this world, a terrible accident happened when an aeroplane came down in an adjoining field. The farm next to ours had been taken over by the Royal Air Force during the Second World War, with operations from Tempsford Airport remaining a well-kept secret. The airfield was being used for covert missions, whilst flying moonlight operations into enemy-occupied Europe.

Local villagers were ignorant of its real activities. On the other hand, it must have been apparent that something was going on, with the terrifying sound of bombers taking off in the middle of the night. And a worrying sight for our family when these huge monsters flew right in front of our bedroom windows in the early hours of the morning. Being so close, they blocked out the light.

Then on February 14th 1945, at around two o'clock in the afternoon, there was an almighty noise from the direction of Tempsford airfield. So what happened that day? Apparently, a

Mustang P51-B fighter bomber from the US Air Force was flying unauthorised over Tempsford airfield and collided, mid-air, with an RAF Short Stirling bomber from 161 Squadron, which was returning to the airport. The collision caused the Short Stirling to be cut in two, and all aircrew from both aircraft were tragically killed that day.

This also caused a bit of a catastrophe for our family, as shrapnel came down onto our roof, leaving a gaping hole in the ceiling. Hence, twinkle, twinkle little star, was much more than a nursery rhyme that night. Awaking with the larks next morning, we had lots of other things to take our mind off this unfortunate incident, and life for us children quickly returned to normal.

A year or so later, I remember quite clearly another occurrence when something major happened in one of our fields. But my family, believing I was too young to understand, shut me inside. All the same, I was determined to be part of the action, so I climbed onto a stool and escaped by lifting the heavy latch on the old oak door. Peering round the corner of the house, I could see a great deal of action going on and lots of people rushing around. Then as I was about to get closer, suddenly a pair of arms scooped me up and took me inside. Now I'll never know what actually happened that day!

It must been about this time that I became aware of Tessa, our much loved Old English sheepdog. Inquisitive to know what was making such a commotion, she stuck her head over the side of my pram one day, and from then on became my friend. But it was only because Dad wouldn't let me have a pony, that I tried riding Tessa instead. Being a working dog, she wasn't overly impressed, and without a saddle to hold me tight, I took a tumble into a pile of muck.

Despite this incident, I wasn't happy that she had to sleep in a kennel outside the front door, as I thought she might be lonely and afraid of the dark and decided she should come to bed with me instead. My parents' wouldn't allow this. I wasn't sure why!

Even worse, Tessa was afraid of thunderstorms, and on one such occasion, being so terrified, she leapt straight through the kitchen window. The sound of breaking glass in the middle of the night was somewhat alarming, and from then on she was allowed into the house during such storms. To stop her roaming, Dad tied her to the hallstand. But Tessa, unused to being indoors, relieved her boredom by chewing on the wooden knobs, and although she's long gone the evidence of her tooth marks remain to this day.

Tessa's role was to protect the house and to help Dad round up the cows; this she did twice a day. She was also my friend, and I didn't want to share her with anyone else. Including my sister, Angela, who was cute and angelic: not mischievous and naughty like me. She had dark curly hair and big brown eyes and over the years, was always my father's favourite. Perhaps it was my imagination and simply appeared that way. Or maybe it was because she had Mother's demeanour and reminded him of his lost love?

Being very young, I wasn't aware of this favouritism, and anyway, Dad made up for it by taking me with him on the farm. Supposedly, it was to keep me out of trouble, although it didn't work all the time. Like when things got a bit out of hand as I swung on a big farm gate, when suddenly and without warning it collapsed upon me. I had been warned that such behaviour would end in disaster, but I couldn't resist the temptation and subsequently suffered the consequence of my actions.

The adults were rushing around panic-stricken and wondering what to do next, and because they weren't sure whether I had any broken bones, I was whisked away to hospital. This was a terrifying ordeal for a small girl, and with many strange faces staring down at me, I screamed and kicked and created such a commotion as they struggled to hold me on the x-ray table.

Luckily, my misfortune was better than my brother's, as when helping to dig the garden one day, the fork slipped and went through his foot. Despite the pain, he was braver than me and didn't cause such a fuss.

After Robert's mishap, it wasn't until the age of two years and four months, that the next memorable episode in my life came round. Christmas, and the one I remember the most. Angela and I, being the two youngest, shared a bedroom and a huge bed, and every night before going to sleep we said our prayers.

We had been promised that if we were really good, Santa would visit in the night to bring our presents. So we said extra-long prayers, if only to make sure he didn't forget. Then we opened out sacks out and hung them on the posts at the end of our bed.

There was a massive fireplace in our bedroom, so we knew that Santa, unless he was really fat, would easily be able to climb down our chimney. A fire was only lit if very cold, but definitely not tonight, otherwise Santa might get his breeches burnt. I don't know if he liked mince pies, but we left some anyway, and they weren't there next morning, so I think they met with his approval.

Angela and I awoke really early, it was pitch-dark, and we had to fumble around in search of our presents. The feel of crinkly paper: oh happy Christmas Day! Santa had been to see us - our extra-long prayers had been answered. Not wasting any time, we tore open the wrapping. The excitement for two little girls was almost too much to bear. Our squeals of delight woke our parents, who promptly tucked us into bed again. They said we had to wait for Robert and MaryAnn to open their presents. But it was too late - we had already torn the wrapping off ours, even though we'd got it wrong and opened each others.

Grandpa Wilfred came round later that day to have a mince-pie and a spot of something stronger than the usual cup of tea. I loved my grandpa. We didn't see too much of him over the years, so I hoped that my big hug would last until his next visit, if only to make sure he didn't forget who I was.

Father never talked about his parents – our grandparents – and we never really found out much about Father's life, either. Throughout my childhood and beyond, it was never discussed. It was almost like a secret that he didn't want to share with anyone else. And he only talked fleetingly about the short time spent with our mother. So did he find it too difficult and painful to look back? Or perhaps, he had feelings of guilt that he was away when she needed him most?

Locked in the Bathroom
Because I was a mischievous child, I suppose it was fairly natural that I had a few scrapes and skirmishes, such as the time when I was stranded in the bathroom for hours and hours. That's because I managed to bolt the door – to make sure nobody came in whilst I was on the loo. I knew that's what you were meant to do – my parents did, so why shouldn't I?

13

We had a nice big bathroom though. So whilst waiting to be rescued I ran the taps till the water ran dry and flushed the loo at least twenty times. Then I switched the light on and off, on and off, on and off, until finally the bulb went pop!

How could I have done such a silly thing? I must have grown taller, as I had not been able to reach the lock before. Or did I stand on a stool? I can't quite remember. There was much ado to get me out, or rather for them to get in, until in the end a ladder was put to the window. At the sound of breaking glass I cowered in the corner, nevertheless, I was jolly relieved they had come to my rescue.

After that escapade, and to stop me getting into mischief, whenever possible, Father took me with him in the wagon. Not only did I keep him good company, but it also gave me the opportunity to practise my singing. I don't think it was a duet though, as I never heard my father sing. Not even a whistle. Because I wasn't very good at learning the words of a song, I sang the same lyrics, over and over. Well, at least it kept Dad's attention on the road ahead.

He wouldn't take me to Spitalfields market in London though; he said it was too far for a small child. But I could have helped him spend some of his money, as the princely sum of three hundred pounds was his reward for a lorry load of peas.

When not out and about with my father I could easily entertain myself, as there were many wondrous things to do on our farm. Even so, I preferred having someone to play with and was happier when my siblings came home from school – though quite soon there would be a new baby, and I wouldn't be so alone.

My father was a hard-working farmer and because we had electricity on our farm, he was one of the early pioneers who milked cows with the new milking machine. Previously this job had been done by hand, but much time and labour was saved with this latest method of extracting milk from the cow. And because farming was an important industry during the Second World War, as food was needed to feed the nation, Dad was exempt from conscription.

Furthermore, with many young men having gone to fight, land girls were drafted in to become the new workforce for the farmer. Many of them were town and city girls and it was a big change to their lives. Particularly, as they were doing work the men would normally have done, and they became an invaluable source of labour. We had several of these young girls, including Pamela, who was attracted by Dad's modern outlook and farming methods. Not only did Pamela work on the farm, she also helped Mother in the house and occasionally looked after me. In so doing, she was easing the burden of being a farmer's wife in the 1940s. Especially, as this lifestyle was a big change for my mother. In the parental home she had been used to maids doing the housework, but here at Rectory Farm, there was no such help. The laundry alone was a huge task. Done by hand, it was heavy manual work for someone with four young children and another on the way.

Then there was Percy, our lovely old farmhand. How strange that none of my siblings remember him. Or was he a figment of my childhood imagination? But of course not, how could he have been? I remember the day he gave me some sweets, saying, 'Make sure you share them with the others when they return from school.' It was not my intention, but they looked so tempting I had to try them out. Then by the time my siblings arrived home it was much too late, as somehow, they disappeared. Maybe, they went into my tummy!

Searching for Dreams

Father was a successful farmer, but yearned to own his own farm, and it was to the West Country that he went in search of his dream. But whilst away, a terrible tragedy had occurred back home, and because he was travelling to different places in the region, trying to contact him was difficult. In the end, the British Broadcasting Corporation had to transmit SOS radio messages to track him down.

Mother, who was then seven months pregnant, had been milking the cows when she became unwell. The doctor had been out to see her the day before, but all he said was, 'Take an aspirin and go to bed...,' which is easier said than done, when you have four young children and the cows to milk.

When the ambulance duly arrived to take our mother to hospital, before leaving she said to Pamela, 'Will you look after the children for me?' Pamela was happy to oblige, promising that she would take care of us – a promise she took very seriously indeed.

15

Me, Robert, MaryAnn and Angela

The four of us: Robert, MaryAnn, Angela and me, were lined up to watch as our mother was put into the ambulance. Still under the age of three, I couldn't understand why I was being left behind, so I chased after the ambulance to stop her from going away. But she didn't have chance to say goodbye as she died soon afterwards, along with our unborn baby brother or sister.

Father was in shock, as he had been away searching for dreams, but came home to a nightmare and utterly distraught that his true love had passed away. Not only that, he now had four young children to look after. However, the family rallied round and we were sent to various aunts and uncles.

Nevertheless, our stay with relatives was brief as Pamela was willing to help Dad out. She was extremely young, barely twenty years old, and despite pleas from her family, several months later she married my father. Having promised our mother that she would look after us, she was keeping her word.

At the time, I was much too young to realise what an enormous impact this would have on my life. Even though I had tried to stop my mother from going away, I still had Pamela, who I adored. After all, she had looked after me when Mum was busy or tired, and now she was comforting me and promising that she would take care of me and my brother and sisters.

Society, though, had a way of making life difficult for people who crossed over the boundaries of social class, as despite my parents having come from similar backgrounds, Mother's family were not happy when she married my father. What was it they were not happy about? Nobody gave us an answer, but it caused many years of dissension in the family. And now Father was marrying Pamela, there was opposition from his family too. But we were moving from the area and out of reach of anything more than the odd letter or card. Perhaps this was Dad's intention all along?

Chapter Two – Moving To Cornwall

Because I was so young, moving from Rectory Farm was another big adventure, and at first, Cornwall was a name without any particular meaning, until we arrived and found out that it was going to be quite different from our previous home. But more importantly, I wasn't told that Tessa was being left behind, until it was too late to kick up a fuss. So why did Father take us away from friends and relatives at such a crucial time? Maybe, the transaction had been done before our mother's death and then it was too late to back out of the deal. Or perhaps it was a 'gentleman's agreement' – the sort of arrangement commonly used in the 1940s.

On the other hand, Father always loved Cornwall, so was this still his dream? Furthermore, having buried our mother close by in the beautiful and tranquil cemetery in Bodmin, clearly it was his intention to make this our permanent home.

We wouldn't be able to play hide-and-seek any more as the house was much too small. But it wasn't only the size: lighting was from paraffin lamps, water had to be pumped from the well in the back garden and bedrooms shared. We were also told, although it never actually happened, that the kitchen floor, being lower than the rest of the house, flooded if it rained too much.

It was in this same kitchen that my new mum tried to drown me. Well, that's how it seemed to me. Terrified of getting soapy water in my eyes whilst having my hair washed, I screamed and yelled and tried hiding under the table when it became my turn. Believing that if I made a big commotion, Mum might give up, and then I could escape to the garden. Only rarely did I get away with being such a nuisance.

Soon after moving in it became apparent there was too much of everything to fit inside this little house, and because Father wasn't a materialistic person, valuable items may well have been left behind at Rectory Farm.

And if it didn't fit in, then he may well have chopped the legs off or even cut it in half, with no serious thought to damage being done to beautiful pieces of furniture.

But most of all, I remember so well the mice that lived behind the skirting boards in the front bedroom, as there were many little holes, just big enough for a mouse to get through. I thought it really good fun putting marbles down the holes, to see if I could flush them out. I was very young at the time, and small furry mice didn't bother me, unlike Angela, who was terrified of these tiny creatures.

I also remember the lovely oil painting of a fine horse. In its beautiful gilt frame, it hung proudly on the wall overlooking the dining room table. At some stage someone put a chair leg through the canvas, causing a big hole, but it never got repaired, as there were too many other important things to worry about. I do not know what happened to it – it just disappeared. Apparently, it was a Stubbs, but at the time, that would have meant little to me.

Before our move, we visited Grandpa Wilfred and Aunty Betty, who was our step-grandmother and Wilfred's new wife. She was very young and pretty, so I'm not sure what Father made of his new stepmother, who was barely the age of his sister. Standing in the doorway of my grandfather's house, I was entranced, as I could see many beautiful things adorning his home: numerous ornaments, knick-knacks and many lovely items of furniture.

I was very young, so how could I have been aware of such things? After all, these weren't toys or dolls, they were things that belonged to the adult world, but the memories remain vivid for all time. It also made me aware of the many treasures belonging to the family, but they were wasted on my father. If a silver salver was suitable for feeding the dog or an old chair could be chopped up for firewood, then as far as he was concerned, so be it.

Following our move to Cornwall and Grandpa's move to Cambridge, contact with him all but ceased. It's a good job I gave him a big hug before leaving Rectory Farm, because I didn't see him again, as he passed away just before I was ten years old. Father probably paid him a visit in-between, but he never told us where he went. Whenever we asked, 'Where are you going?' he would usually reply, 'To see a man about a dog.'

Perhaps, it was the lush grass that attracted Dad to the West Country, as it was perfect for producing high milk yields. And to ensure everything was ready for the cows, he had spent a great deal of time making preparations prior to our move. In contrast to Rectory Farm there was no electricity, so the cows had to be milked by hand, which was much more labour-intensive than the milking machine.

My dad was incredibly talented when it came to working with his hands, as he had built a new milking parlour, and a storeroom. All the same, I couldn't understand why I wasn't allowed into this store, until one day, I spied Dad's working ferrets and was told if I stuck my finger inside their cage, they might mistake it for a tasty morsel. Not being too keen on the idea of becoming a 'tasty morsel' I didn't try it out, as that would have hindered my ability to play with my brother and sisters.

Next to the ferrets home were some tall steps jutting out from the side of the milking parlour. I was intrigued, as these steps went nowhere, apart from upwards. Whatever their purpose, it didn't bother us, as we made best use of them by running to the top and leaping over the edge to the ground below.

There were no railings at the top of these steps either, and a sheer drop on both sides. Amazingly there were no serious accidents, despite being much too steep for a small child of four or five years old. But we were very courageous and found the most adventurous things to do, making games up as we went along. There was no pampering or cosseting for us. We were the fearless four!

Then I did something dreadful one day. Even though I loved animals, I took a kitten to the top of these steps and dropped it over the edge. Fortunately, little kitty had nine lives. Nevertheless, I lived with the guilt for a very long time, and vowed never to do such a horrid thing again.

Shortly after our arrival a new Dutch barn was built, and life on the farm seemed almost complete, until one night a wild storm blew it down again. I have some vague recollection of this happening, but remember it most when loaded to the top with straw and bales of hay. It was such fun clambering to the top of the barn, and then sliding all the way back down to the bottom again.

This activity must have happened unknown to our parents, as it was a perilous game for young children to play. But I was a real tomboy, and whatever the others were doing I was determined to participate, even when they didn't want me to – and then, I was jolly determined not to be left out. They wouldn't be able to share my fifth birthday present though: my new baby sister, Sophia. Mum had promised that she was especially for me before starting school.

Whilst Mum was in hospital, our step-grandparents came to help look after us, but with a shortage of bedrooms I was confined to a cot in my parents' room. Then one night I heard my father sobbing inconsolably. What was it that had made him so distressed? I didn't ask why, and didn't say anything to anyone else, either. Was he weeping for our mother, his true love, as he had lost her so tragically? Or maybe it was because things hadn't been going too well on the farm? Whatever it was, he was very sad, and I didn't comfort him, but I was just a small child and didn't know how to respond to his tears.

The incident was forgotten, when after two weeks in hospital Mum arrived home with the new baby. Peering into the crib, we were anxious to find out which one of us she looked like. But we were quite unprepared to see that this latest addition to the family had bright ginger hair. So I asked Mum, 'Where do babies come from?' She promptly replied, 'From under the gooseberry bush.' I looked under the gooseberry bush, I searched everywhere – all around the garden and the hedgerows too – but none were to be found. Someone was telling me lies!

Now that I had reached the age of five, my school days were almost upon me. Prior to living in Cornwall my three older siblings were being privately educated, and MaryAnn and Angela had ballet lessons too. However, circumstances were different now, and so apart from MaryAnn, Robert, Angela and I attended the local school.

Because we were living in the depths of rural Cornwall, there was only one school for the area, and that was at St Juliot. Basically, it was a large house with one classroom, which was used for infants up until school leaving age. Imagine that – all ages in one classroom!

I wasn't keen on the idea of school, but being in the same classroom with Robert and Angela helped, even though we were parted by way of a thick curtain. Consequently, there was no chance of a quick peep, not even to see what they were doing in their lessons. I have no recollection of this first school, apart from sitting on a long bench in the front row with a slate and a piece of chalk. So what did I learn? I don't remember that either. But I bet I would have preferred to have been playing outside.

For those children who were about to leave school, many of them were a mere fourteen years of age, and if farm children, often went to work on the land. And with tin mines being part of the Cornish heritage, others may have gone down the mines to work.

MaryAnn, since the age of seven, had attended a convent school in Bedford with two of her cousins. Before leaving, or when arriving home at the end of term, she would be wearing her lovely uniform: a smart pleated dress and a big straw boater hat; and of course there was the trunk, which held all her worldly possessions. I was so envious of her!

School life was quite different for Robert, Angela and me; to start with, we had a journey of several miles to school. Often, when Mum drove into Camelford or Boscastle to do her weekly shop, she dropped us off on the way – even so, we found riding on the back of the milk lorry a more exciting mode of transport.

Early every morning the lorry arrived to collect the milk churns, and after loading up we sat on the back of the lorry with our legs dangling over the edge. It may well have been dangerous if going over a big hole or bump in the road, but it didn't occur to us that tumbling over the edge might have been painful.

Upon arriving at the school gates the driver unloaded the crates containing the quarter-pint bottles of milk, which in 1949, was every child's entitlement. During the winter months the milk often froze, and to ensure it melted in time for our morning break, the crates were put on top of the giant stove to thaw out. There were no cooked school meals in such a rural area either, so all children took a packed lunch. To keep us well fed and nourished, Mum made scrumptious homemade Cornish pasties. She was such a good cook.

Going home at the end of the day was more of a problem than our morning ride on the milk lorry. Usually we walked, but not on the roads, as that was the long way round. Instead, a short cut across the fields was our best option. I was only five and a bit, and it seemed such a long way after a tiring day at school. But there was no dilly-dallying; we knew tea would be ready: freshly baked scones and lovely homemade cakes were a treat worth rushing home for.

One day as I sped along the footpath, trying to keep up with Robert and Angela, who were being really horrid, as they had left me behind, I was suddenly stopped in my tracks. Standing there in front of me were two burly lads. Unexpectedly and without warning, they swept me off my feet, and started swinging me off the ground by my arms and legs and laughing hysterically. I thought my torment would never end as they swung me to and fro. Then Robert heard my cries for help and came to my rescue. This was a terrifying ordeal and one I've never forgotten. How cruel they were to do such a thing to a young child. I wish I could confront them now!

All the same, at times we were naughty too, and one of our tricks whilst walking home after school was to sabotage the gin traps. By putting sticks into the mechanism the trap snapped closed, in so doing, the life of a rabbit was spared. On one such occasion, Angela accidentally got her fingers caught and was lucky they weren't severed from her hands, as these brutal contraptions could have broken her bones. Only later were they banned for good.

An even worse dilemma was when the ford – which was a short distance from our house – flooded, and we were unable to cross to the other side. The fragile wooden bridge was no match for the strong flowing current, which could easily have swept us away.

But it wasn't always that bad and sometimes on our way home from school we picked bunches of wild flowers. During the summer months the hedgerows were full of red campions, foxgloves and many others, which we gathered until our arms were full. Then we rushed home with our surprise, a special gift for Mum, to show how much we cared. We had been taught to look after nature and only pick the flowers we wanted, as there were many animals and insects living in the hedgerows and fields, and this was their home too.

Our school wasn't easy to find if you didn't know where to look, unless you came upon it by chance, as it was tucked away on one of those narrow Cornish lanes. With grass growing in the middle of the lane, you'd think they were farm tracks if you weren't familiar with the terrain; although that wasn't a problem for us, as Dad's old Ford car probably knew its own way around the lanes near our farm.

Then there was the matter of the Cornish hedge, which, being so tall and wide, were almost impossible to see over. Apparently it's for a reason, as they provide shelter from the Atlantic gales, shade in the summer months, and a home for the insects, birds and wildlife to enjoy for the rest of the year – but try telling that to a small child.

With few tall hedges surrounding our farm, it was very exposed, which meant we could see for many miles over open countryside, and we took advantage of this beauty on lovely summer days, with long leisurely walks around the lanes. Even though Mum wasn't a true country girl, she knew lots of different things, and taught us the names of wild flowers and poisonous plants that we mustn't touch. And if by chance we wanted a wee, then we needed to find a large dock leaf and then a tree or bush to hide behind.

Those lovely walks were such a joy as we held hands, arms swinging, with skylarks singing so sweetly above. And we joined in too and sang our favourite songs. Mum had such a beautiful voice, and I loved to listen to her singing, with one of my favourites being 'Ten Green Bottles' as it taught us how to count backwards:

'Ten green bottles hanging on a wall, if one green bottle was to accidentally fall, there would be nine green bottles hanging on the wall, and if one green bottle was to accidentally fall, there would be eight green bottles hanging on the wall...'

Snail Race Bridge

24

Another of our interests was the railway line, and only a few minutes away at the bottom of our fields. Being a major link from London to Padstow, the trains took country produce back to the big city. We loved to watch as the train sped along the track and then as it disappeared under the bridge, it emerged the other side amidst a huge plume of smoke. Passengers often waved to us, and we waved back frantically until the train had disappeared from sight.

The bridge over the railway track was also a place of amusement. Ignoring all warnings, we often climbed on the end and ran along the parapet. It was great fun, and we saw no danger.

An even bigger thrill was when Snail Race Bridge and the surrounding lanes were being resurfaced, when at great speed we rushed over to watch the steam roller doing its job. To and fro it went, over and over, again and again, rolling the surface down until it was quite smooth. There was even more excitement when we persuaded the driver to give us a ride. Was it the sound that only a steam engine makes, or perhaps the smell? Whatever it was, we were spellbound by this magnificent beast.

Father often talked about the steam traction engines used on the farm when he was a boy. His job was to rise early and before breakfast stoke the engine to get steam up ready for the farm labourers. Perhaps, this was the start of his love affair with steam trains, and in particular, the Flying Scotsman. With the railway track running through his fields at Rectory Farm, Dad knew exactly the time of day this iconic engine passed by. And now here in Cornwall, with the track on his doorstep, maybe he was rekindling those boyhood memories.

Possibly this was another of his reasons for wanting to live in rural Cornwall, given that our little house was nothing like the one we had left behind. It was very basic, even for 1948, and without the services we had become used to, oil lamps and candles being used for the purpose of lighting. Oh, those lovely old brass lanterns! Despite their charm, we thought they were old fashioned and out of date, and threw them out as soon as we could.

There was no running water either; our water came from a well at the bottom of the back garden. One day MaryAnn nearly had her ear bitten off by an unruly sheepdog when she was lifting water from the well to give him a drink. Even so, Pooch was a very clever little dog. When Father shut the bedroom window in the morning, usually around four or five o'clock, it was a signal for Pooch to go and round up the cows. His job was to bring them to the parlour, so that Dad could do the milking before the lorry arrived to collect the churns.

Our farm was a great deal smaller than our previous farm. There was enough land for the cows to graze and a bit over for sowing crops, but the landscape, climate and farming methods were very different from Bedfordshire. So why did Dad decide upon such a secluded and isolated place? It was never talked about, and we continue to speculate as to the reason why.

What's more, with the farm being a thousand feet above sea level, it could be very bleak and frequently shrouded in mist, and sometimes it seemed as if our heads were almost touching the clouds. But on clear days there was a view all the way to the sea, and that was a lovely sight. With the seaside at Boscastle only a few miles away, on summer days I ran around on the beach in my birthday suit, with the freedom that only a five-year-old child can do.

Nearer to home, our place was surrounded by peace and tranquillity, beautiful waterfalls, lush green meadows and stunning valleys, making it truly special. On the other hand, the narrow country lanes and steep hills would put all but the tenacious off viewing these places of interest.

And it was on one of those narrow and very steep lanes where we had a bit of a problem, when one day our little car, with not a lot of horsepower, didn't want to go to the top of a 1 in 4 hill. Father had to reverse back down and then a carload of children leapt out to help reduce the load. Starting again, he put his foot hard down on the accelerator, and without too much of a struggle got to the top.

He was waiting very impatiently for us to arrive, but it is hard work walking up a 1 in 4 hill, even when you are a child. So as not to annoy him further, we quickly clambered into the car to ensure we weren't left behind, as we wouldn't be able to catch up once he started freewheeling down the other side. This was normal practice for Father, as he was always looking for ways to be thrifty, saving money being his forte in life.

During the summer months we often took leisurely evening strolls around the fields, as Dad was keen to inspect damage done by the rabbits. Most people, if not from the land, will not have heard of the dreadful gin trap, but rabbits, being prolific breeders, can devastate crops in no time at all, and it was important to keep them under control.

Twice a week the 'Trap Man' duly arrived with his horse and cart and set traps outside the burrows. Nevertheless, it was an unfortunate demise for the poor little bunnies, as when the trap closed, it was not unusual for a rabbit to lose a leg, and then to escape to some untold suffering and misery

Because we children were upset by the use of this killing machine, Mum often tried to set off or even remove some of the traps, thus sparing death and pain, but with the trap man being paid for this service, Father would be extremely annoyed. After all, it was necessary to save his crops, and rabbits also provided us with a free source of food. Furthermore, the trap man made his money by sending the rabbits on the steam train to London.

Watching my father skin a rabbit was amazing, he had such speed and dexterity, although years of practice meant he had perfected this skill, and Mum knew every way to turn a rabbit into a tasty meal.

Just as damaging, albeit in a different way, are snails – as they can munch through newly sown veggie plants overnight, with not a trace of greenery left come next morning. The thrushes, blackbirds and toads helped us out, but even they couldn't eat enough to stop the devastation caused by this garden pest.

Despite being unpopular, snails were a source of enjoyment for us children. Not to eat – although some folk in other parts of the world may well regard them as a delicacy, but ours were for snail racing events. Not the big, brown, ugly ones, either. We only wanted the pretty snails, and spent many hours hunting around in the greenery and undergrowth seeking out the most beautiful and exquisitely marked. Yellow and red, and green and blue – the delicate colours swirling around their dainty little shell houses looked so very pretty.

When we had found the perfect specimen, racing across the old railway bridge began. Snail Race Bridge was a place of great excitement and entertainment for us children throughout the summer months. After a while the snails became exhausted, so we fed them with lettuce we found in the garden, to ensure they were in prime condition and ready for their next race.

Then whilst the snails conserved their energy for another day, we had to find something else to entertain us, although generally, this wasn't a problem as there was much to do on the farm. A great deal of our time was spent exploring the countryside and learning about insects, butterflies and wild flowers. We knew the names of them all, as such things were important for a country child, and it expanded our knowledge of what was happening outside our own front door.

Saying Goodbye
We hadn't been at our Cornish home for long before a lot of bad luck caused us to move from the farm. Due to extreme weather conditions Dad's crops were ruined, and having tried to rescue them, he wasn't paid compensation by the government, as had been received by other farmers in the area. With little capital to tide him over and without food for the animals, he had no choice - we had to go.

He was extremely upset when his Ayrshire cows, which were his pride and joy, went to new homes. Before we left, and to help Dad out financially, we dug the fields for worms to sell to the local fishermen. Pretty snails didn't cause me a problem. But worms! I screamed in protestation as they squirmed and wriggled in the palm of my hand. Then Mum said that it would help Dad out, so I shut my eyes tightly as I put them in the bucket.

Prior to leaving, Sophia was baptised, with the service being held in the pretty church at St Juliot. This was the same church that the writer, Thomas Hardy met Emma, his future wife, whilst surveying it for restoration. Not that it made any difference to Sophia, or indeed any of us, as we were much too young to be aware of its significance.

We were also ignorant of the changes about to take place in our lives. But that wasn't to last, as once the celebrations were over, tea chests were delivered in advance of moving day. It was a family affair as we all got involved with the packing, whilst taking great care to wrap precious items in copious amounts of newspaper, to ensure a safe journey to our next destination.

When the Pickfords removal van duly arrived on the morning of our departure and as I watched our possessions being loaded in, I knew I didn't want to leave. So I went to ground! Eventually they found me hiding in the gardens and I was extracted from the undergrowth. Then we parted with our Cornish dream and moved on to a new life.

Chapter Three – Sent to Coventry

Initially, the family moved to a temporary place in Dawlish, but soon afterwards, I was despatched to stay with my Aunt Win, Uncle Dick and Colin my cousin, at Wyvern Crescent in Coventry.

Despite leaving early in the morning, it was a long drive to Coventry, and I knew Dad would be ready for a cup of tea. Upon arrival at Aunt Win's, she made us a fresh pot of tea and some cucumber sandwiches. The bread was thinly sliced and had the crusts cut off. But we didn't do things like that in our house, as my father would regard it as being extremely wasteful.

Then I spotted what I had been looking for – whoopee! My favourites: marshmallows all covered in chocolate. This was pure luxury, as back home we didn't have anything that was not homemade or grown in the garden. So I made this delicious treat last for as long as possible, savouring every lick of the chocolate, and then, the marshmallow within.

This must have been bribery, even if I was too young to realise it at the time. And having stayed with my aunt when I was much younger, I wasn't unduly concerned about being away from my brother and sisters. 'Only until the family settles into our new home,' is what my father said. Naively, I thought that meant for just a few weeks, so it seemed rather strange when they started talking about 'going to school.' Surely they couldn't be referring to me? Particularly, if I was only going to be with them for such a short time; I'd been thinking it was an opportunity to have a holiday away from school, not attend another.

Nevertheless, I would have to do what I was told, because my aunt, although very loving, didn't stand for any nonsense. When Dad brought my little leather suitcase into the house, I'd suddenly changed my mind about staying. Perhaps my sisters weren't quite so horrid after all, but it was too late. Father never messed about when it came to timing – as quickly as we arrived – so he departed.

Aunty Win took the suitcase upstairs. It had all my possessions: my clothes, my pyjamas and my special teddy bear. Looking around the room, all of a sudden I became quite sad, as I wouldn't have anyone to cuddle up to in bed. Back in the family home, I shared a bedroom and a bed with my two older sisters, but here I had my own special room.

All the same, it was a perfect sized room for a small child, with a tiny bed and a tiny set of drawers. My aunt had clearly given great thought to ensuring I was happy with my very own space. Even so, it was rather like a large doll's house as everything appeared to be in miniature. I should have loved this new adventure, except I wasn't used to sleeping on my own, and would often be afraid.

One advantage, however, my room was at the front of the house overlooking the road, and until midnight there was a light. Every evening the 'Lamp Man' came to ignite the gas lantern in the street outside my room. This gave a glimmer of light, and as the shadows flickered and danced around the room, it helped lull me to sleep.

I was little more than six years old when I was sent to Coventry, and even though my cousin Colin was very kind and caring and like a brother to me, I still missed my family. Aunt Win had wanted to adopt me, but Father said, 'You can have her until she's fifteen, and then I want her back.' This, of course, they did not want to do, so although my visit was meant to be for 'a short time only', I think I was there for nearly a year.

It didn't take long to realise that I had left the best of my school years in Cornwall, and it was with great reluctance that I agreed to attend school with Colin. Being several years older, he held my hand all the way. Was it to give me extra confidence? Or more than likely, to make sure I didn't try and escape.

The classrooms were like temporary wooden huts, so I'm sure the proper school must have been bombed in the war when Coventry came under attack. Not only that, it was much larger and more intimidating than my school at St. Juliot. And bewildering too, as everything else in my life had changed. I remember little of this time, apart from deciding that school wasn't for me. Nevertheless, Aunt Win told me in a matter of fact manner that I must attend, as it was good for me academically.

Despite my reluctance to attend school, it was more enjoyable in the winter when the pavements became icy. With the soles of my shoes being made of leather they were terrific for sliding on ice, although for some unknown reason, Aunt Win wasn't happy about this. On reflection, perhaps it had something to do with the fact that it made a hole in the sole of my shoe.

All the same, if I had been at home, Dad would have put Phillips stick-on-soles on my shoes to make them last longer. He had all the equipment to do a first-class job, as prolonging the wear-ability of our shoes saved him a lot of money. Nearly every family did it, except Aunt Win. She didn't do things like that, so I had to suffer the consequence of my actions.

I was never really a bully at school, preferring to be peaceful and not to get into a fight, although something must have triggered a reason for me bashing another girl as I walked home from school one day. Then when she started crying, I fled the scene of my crime. What caused this outburst? I do not know. Terrified of being found out, I was very careful not to do such a horrid thing again.

But at least I had weekends to look forward to, as Uncle Dick loved to play golf, and every Saturday morning he went to the golf course and often took me with him. I can't remember if this was supposed to be an enjoyable experience, or to get me out of the way of Aunt Win for a while, or maybe, a punishment. I'm not sure how he managed to put up with me either, as I loved doing cartwheels and handstands and messing about, whilst he was trying to hit small balls into what appeared to be an even smaller hole. He was so patient though, and didn't get angry. Perhaps he understood that he was my family now, and I needed his love.

Even better was my first experience of riding on a bus; a double-decker. Oh what joy! Leaping onto the bottom step, I ran upstairs as fast as I could, and rushed to the front seat to make sure I got the best view. We didn't ride on buses back home, so these trips into Coventry gave me a great deal of pleasure, making my stay with Aunt Win much more enjoyable.

A Dolly for Christmas

I had been with my aunt and uncle for much more than 'a few weeks' when Christmas Eve came around. Nevertheless, it was an exciting time - as I had sent my request to Santa in advance to make sure he got it right. Also, because Colin was a choirboy we had to attend the church service. Then as we walked home I remember more than anything else, the huge array of coloured lights and illuminations, as we didn't have such displays where I came from. But when the clock struck midnight I knew I was in trouble. Not only was it terribly late for a small girl who was normally asleep by seven o'clock, but having been told if I wasn't tucked up in bed when Santa came round, he might go somewhere else instead.

Even though I tried staying awake to ask Santa, 'Please bring me a doll,' tiredness got in the way, and I fell asleep before he arrived. But he didn't let me down. Awaking early next morning, I opened my eyes, and I knew my prayers had been answered as lying next to me on my pillow was a little doll.

Colin and me with our special presents

33

She was so beautiful – with pretty, blonde curly hair and wearing the most gorgeous pale green outfit. I loved her instantly. And because I was so excited, I couldn't think of an appropriate name, so I called her 'Dolly'.

Colin had a cowboy suit for his Christmas present, and side-by-side we stood, he in his fancy outfit and me cuddling my precious Dolly, and a photograph was taken. This is the only proof I have of this special moment, as Dolly went to a different home later in my life.

During the holidays we visited Grandpa Cross and two spinster aunts who lived with him. Whilst there, I was allowed to play his gramophone, which was a great privilege, as we didn't have one like that at home. With its huge brass horn and wind-up handle, it was very impressive. Then, with Dolly by my side, I sat on the windowsill in a room upstairs and played my favourite song many times. I must have driven them mad! It was all about a girl called Alice and the changing of the guard, and in my world of make-believe, I was Alice at Buckingham Palace:

> *'They're changing the guard at Buckingham Palace.*
> *Christopher Robin went down with Alice.*
> *Alice is marrying one of the guards.*
> *'A soldier's life is terribly hard', says Alice...'*

It didn't matter that I couldn't remember all the lines of the song, as I just sang the same ones over and over. Then when the record came to the end, I had to rewind the gramophone before being able to play it again.

If I'd been at home with my brother and sisters, Christmas would have been different to the one I'd just had. And with six of us, our Christmas stockings had fruit and sweets, and perhaps a few trinkets – other presents tended to be shared, such as board games. These were a favourite when visiting our cousins in Oxfordshire as the Monopoly board always came out after lunch. The grown-ups were more than happy, as it kept us occupied for many hours.

Being so young, I never questioned why I was staying with my aunt and uncle, and anyway, I had little choice in the matter, as it was a time when children did as they were told. And regardless of missing my family, this was a special Christmas for me, as I didn't have to share Dolly with anyone else. Not my big sisters or even my little sisters and when I returned home, she was definitely not for sharing. Being my only worldly possession, she was truly my very own, and I treasured her.

Going Home

With Christmas over, and having spent more than a year with my aunt and uncle, I was becoming a bit of a handful. Perhaps I should have been grateful for all the attention, but a young mind doesn't always think like that, and I'd started to become difficult. I'd also drawn on the walls with crayon in my bedroom, and my aunty wasn't very pleased. So the decision was made - it was time to go home.

I was excited at the prospect of seeing my brother and sisters, as a year was a long time to be away. But there was a problem. I didn't have any shoes! Sliding on ice was all good fun, but having worn holes in the soles of my shoes, all I had to wear was my wellies. And it was with great reluctance, and huge embarrassment, that I got on the coach wearing my wellington boots.

Except, unbeknown to me, not only had my family moved to Wiltshire whilst I had been away, but I was quite unprepared for the surprise that awaited me: another new baby. She had dark hair and big brown eyes and Louise was her name. Everyone kept saying, 'She looks just like Angela' and, 'How pretty she is.'

Unsurprisingly, having been away all this time I expected lots of fuss, but being part of a big family I didn't receive the attention I craved. It was no use sulking either, as that would be ignored. So I had to get on with life as best I could. But worse was to come, the toilet wasn't in the house. Oh no! It was at the bottom of the garden and extremely unpleasant when it was raining and cold, so I wasn't very impressed with this new arrangement.

Staring into the abyss was a horrid thing to do, but somewhat fascinating for a small child, as it appeared to be a great hole in the ground. What's more, if the toilet paper ran out before shopping day, we children were charged with the job of shredding newspaper into small squares. They were then threaded onto a long piece of string and hung at just the right height.

We had a beautiful garden though, and that made up for the dreaded loo. The long footpath swept down to the house and was lined with beautiful flowers: lupins, hollyhocks, tall daises and roses and many more and was such a delight. Father had joined the cricket club, and every Sunday during the summer months he put on his whites and off he went to the village green. With his many years of playing cricket, he was a great asset to his team. My father was a tall, slim, elegant man, and I was really proud of him.

At Bedford School he had been in the rowing team, and participated in many other recreational pursuits and won numerous events throughout his schooldays. He also loved to skate. When he was a lad, the rivers often froze around the fens during the winter months, and he and his sister, Freda, skated along the River Lea from one of their grandfather's farms to another.

Then when he was too old to participate in this sport, he watched ice dancing on television instead. Mostly, I suspect, to watch the pretty young ladies in their skating dresses, as when he was a young man and skating outside, the girls couldn't dress like that or they would more than likely get frostbite.

Having settled in with my family I was able to take Sophia out for nice walks in her pushchair, and it was on one of those glorious summer days whilst out for a stroll, that I had a terrible fright. Suddenly from behind I could hear a thundering sound. Looking round, I could see a horse galloping at great speed down the lane. Not only that, it was heading straight for us! Terrified, I cowered in the ditch. Being such a dreadful shock I was a trembling wreck. But then, and only just in time, I saw Mum, bravely racing down the lane to come to our rescue.

After recovering from this ordeal, a few nights later I had to live through another - a thunderstorm! It was so ferocious that we sat huddled together on the stairs in the middle of the house. On the other hand, MaryAnn loved thunderstorms, so whilst we cowered on the stairs, she sat on the windowsill watching until it passed by.

Unfortunately, we had to get up early next morning as we were off to see Aunty Pegg – our step-grandmother, who was a short, plump, kindly lady. Then there was Uncle Pegg! To a young child he appeared quite formidable, but as he was a policeman, I suppose his temperament fitted him perfectly. Even so, I was a little afraid of him, and more so after knocking a milk bottle off his doorstep and then being threatened with a visit to the police station.

It was not my intention of course, but as we were about to leave, I was jumping on and off the step when the accident happened. Aunty Pegg was extremely annoyed by my clumsiness, 'That's tuppence from your pocket money,' she said. I hid behind Mum, as I thought I was in for a hiding, and was very relieved when we departed.

Heaven Through The Eyes of a Child
The next year or so was quite a blur, as we moved to several different places and I have no recollection of houses or schools. Was there something sinister and horrid happening that my subconscious was blocking it from my mind?

About this time I remember a vision that has remained with me through the years. To this very day I do not know where it was, except that it was sometime before our move to the Cotswolds.

Whilst out with my brother and sisters and going for a stroll in the country, we came upon a wonderful meadow that was full to the brim with clover and wild flowers and so lightly perfumed, it smelt divine.

Being such a beautiful scene I stood there in wonder and amazement, observing this great act of nature, as beauty had no bounds. Surrounded by such perfection I thought I was in heaven.

Throughout my life I have never experienced a sight, or sensation, so vivid and so special, that would leave such a lasting legacy in my memory box. If indeed this was heaven, then I will be happy to go there in time.

Chapter Four - Estcourt Park, Tetbury

Father eventually found a good job as a farm manager at Grange Farm, one of the farms within Estcourt Park; a beautiful private country estate near Tetbury in the Cotswolds. The lovely mellow stone houses, soft rolling hills, woodlands and lakes made it a special place. This was my home for quite some time, and where my heart will always be.

The downside was that I had to attend yet another school, but overall my schooldays became more settled, and the months ahead, for most of the time, were good. Except that wasn't to last, as soon after our move, signs of conflict began to show within my parents' marriage. Perhaps it was because Father couldn't forget our mother: his first love, or the age difference, as they were ten years apart. Or maybe it was because they came from different backgrounds, which in the 1950s, could so often be an issue. If there was love, had it now flown out of the window? It was never talked about. Children were not involved in family matters; they were meant to be seen and not heard, even though we often detected upset and strife.

Nevertheless, I was an inquisitive child, and listened and watched and peered through keyholes, and saw things I shouldn't have seen. Consequently, I knew something was going on, but I put it behind me and carried on as normal.

My mum was so young and pretty and had long silky soft wavy hair, and when working she tied it into a ribbon. If she was unhappy, then she didn't show it, as she was always singing and had a beautiful voice. She could also whistle a tune, a talent that has always evaded me. Her laugh, so soft and lilting, was a joy to hear, and I simply adored her.

She worked hard to keep us clean and well fed, but washing for a large family was an all-day affair. Clean school clothes were laid out on Sunday, ready for Monday morning, and lasted all week. Anything that became soiled before Friday was sorted out with a good brush down.

We had a scullery for doing the washing. Early Monday morning the large copper was filled with cold water, white items went in first, and then the water was gently brought to boiling point. With most items being made of cotton, if boiling didn't work, then a good scrub would remove stubborn stains.

A 'bluebag' was used for the final rinse to give a perfect ice-white finish, after which, the washing was put through the mangle. This was an arduous task, but then Mum had her first proper washing machine, and that had an electric mangle.

The washing line in our back garden seemed to stretch forever. Whenever possible, I sat on the swing watching the clothes blowing in the breeze. I was fascinated, as there appeared to be something quite magical in the way that the washing wafted and fluttered every-which-way. A sudden gust of wind whipped the sheets into frenzy, entangling them the wrong way around the clothes line – much to Mum's annoyance, as she was having coffee and a jam doughnut; a special treat delivered by the baker on Monday morning to help her with the chores.

That wasn't the end of the job either, as the ironing had to be started before the day was out. The big scrub-top kitchen table, with a heavy cloth on top, was used for the ironing process. And if the fabric was too dry, Mum flicked water over it and then after being rolled up for a while, the item was ready for ironing.

The smoothing irons, as there were two, lived on top of the big, black kitchen range: a multi-functioning device that was used for boiling the kettle, drying the clothes and heating the kitchen, as well as warming the back of Mum's legs. So as to ensure the ironing procedure wasn't interrupted, when the first iron became cool, it was put back on the range to be re-heated. To test for temperature Mum spat on the bottom of the iron, and if it sizzled, it was hot enough.

Many items and special finery were starched, including Father's collars and cuffs, which were pure white and ironed to perfection. Then they were placed in his suede collar box, which had pride of place on the glass-knobbed mahogany chest of drawers. Changing the collars and cuffs reduced the need to wash the whole shirt. Not only that, it extended the life of a shirt, with replacement collars and cuffs purchased when the others wore out.

Very soon Mum would have Sophia's school clothes to wash and iron too, as her firth birthday had come around. I was overjoyed! She was my little sister and so pretty, with her freckled face and lovely golden locks and I promised I would do my best to look after her.

To make sure she was okay, I often visited her during break-times, but Sophia obviously didn't like school that much as she was always crying. It upset me to see her looking lonely and isolated, so I often nipped across the road to the tuck shop and bought penny lollypops to keep her happy. This didn't work all the time, and as Mum left home six months later, she wasn't there long enough to get used to her surroundings.

However, a penny was a lot of money, and to keep buying lollies for Sophia I had to keep earning pocket money. Collecting eggs was my favourite job. I would have done it for nothing, but certainly wouldn't tell Dad, as he might have taken me up on my offer. We had a lot of hens and I collected the eggs, even if Mrs Hen was sitting on the nest. With her soft, warm, downy undercarriage sitting tight on a clutch of eggs, I had to be extra careful not to scare her away as I slipped my hand under her tummy and took them, one by one.

There could be six or more eggs, and could easily get cracked by a clumsy chicken. Mrs Hen often became annoyed when disturbed and noisily clucked her way out of the shed. But she might have gone broody, which wasn't allowed, as Father preferred the chickens to lay eggs for him to sell, rather than to have chicks. Then when eggs were plentiful, they were preserved for winter by immersing them in a tall bucket containing a special solution, this process kept them fresh until there was an abundance of eggs once more.

Apart from collecting eggs, we did whatever was required to earn our pocket money. Nevertheless, 'work before play' was a strict rule that we had to abide by at all times. No whining or moaning or jumping around in a temper, we had to get on and do our jobs before going out to play. Sitting for hours picking blackcurrants was more like a punishment than a pleasure for me, and the job I hated most.

The Bank

Father had recently purchased an ultra-modern china cabinet for the dining room; it was quite different from some of the antique furniture that had survived his reckless ways. We called it 'the bank', as the cabinet had four drawers, each one with our name on, and this is where we kept our pocket money. When we had saved enough, we could spend it how we wished, but having been taught to be thrifty we always erred on the side of caution. 'Look after your pennies and the pounds will look after themselves' was one of my father's favourite sayings.

One Christmas, after I had been saving my pennies, we went shopping to buy our gifts. We headed for Woolworths, as unlike many other shops, we knew we would get a good deal. They had a huge selection, but with the counters being so high, I had to stand on tiptoe to see what was on offer. Then I found what I was looking for: a delicate little brooch with the initial 'P'; it was to be a special treat for Mum.

Being very sparkly, it looked like diamonds, but I don't think they were, otherwise it would have cost more than the money I had in my pocket. I proudly purchased this special gift, handing over my hard-earned cash – all of one shilling and three-pence. The nice lady wrapped it in some pretty paper, so all I had to do was hide it away to make sure Mum didn't come upon it by chance, as I didn't want to spoil the surprise on Christmas Day.

We were taught that it doesn't matter what a present costs, '…it's the thought that counts'. I have often thought about this gift and what happened to it. Because Mum left home some months later, I never found out. Did she wear it? Did she keep it in the bottom of a jewellery box, or a drawer? Or did it end up in the bin? After all, it only cost one shilling and three-pence, but the thought meant so much to me.

According to Father, shopping for presents only started a few weeks before the festivities, with Christmas Eve the time for food shopping. Anything made or purchased before this time had to stay on top of the sideboard in the dining room. We could have a look, but definitely no touching.

We loved Christmas; it was such an exciting time. At least Dad allowed us to put the decorations up in advance. Paper chain garlands were purchased as brightly coloured strips of paper, which were then made into a loop in which to put the others through. After many hours of licking and sticking, eventually, we had enough to fill the kitchen, the dining room, the sitting-room and the hallway. All in all, it was a big job. With the main task complete, we found the best holly and strung it across the top of mirrors and pictures, its rosy red berries reminding us Christmas was not far away.

And, in the hope of a quick kiss from someone nice, we strung mistletoe in a prominent place. Well, I knew someone would make best use of it, as I caught Mum kissing the baker one Monday morning. Was it just a peck on the cheek? I am not too sure! She didn't spot me, so I slipped away, tip-toeing out of sight, and pretending I was somewhere else.

Father worked for Captain Smith-Bingham, and every Christmas a turkey was given as part of his annual bonus. One year it was so huge that it wouldn't fit into the oven. Swift action was required! A slice with a sharp knife and the parson's nose came off, resolving the problem for yet another year. Turkey was a special treat and reserved for festivities and with the leftovers served cold for a further week, we were more than happy to wait till next Christmas before having another.

Mum had made the plum puddings several months in advance, as they had to be boiled for many hours in the copper. Then before serving, a silver three-penny or sixpenny piece was inserted somewhere in the middle. We all hoped to be the lucky one to find this special coin, as it meant we would start the New Year feeling quite wealthy. If Dad found the coin in his pudding, then we decided he was cheating, and we wanted a second chance.

There was also the Christmas cake, which I had been eyeing up for some time whilst it sat on the sideboard soaking up the brandy. I was positive that if I dug a bit out from underneath, Mum wouldn't notice. Then I thought - I'd better not. Of course, I could deny all knowledge! Unfortunately, whenever I tried telling a lie I would blush bright red, so they would know it was me. But too late! A thick layer of marzipan stopped me from carrying out my plan.

After Christmas the cake only came out on Sundays as a treat, but at least that meant it would last until Easter. With Christmas Day over, the hard work was about to begin, as come Boxing Day we had to write thank you letters to all our aunts and uncles for our lovely presents. It was a tedious chore, but there was no escaping.

Along with the New Year came the prospect of Spring, even though we always had a big dose of snow before then. This was a problem as far as getting to school was concerned, as walking across fields with snowdrifts of six feet and more was a frightening experience. All the same we had no choice – bad weather was no excuse for taking time off school. So we were more than happy to see baby lambs frolicking in the fields and vibrant spring flowers after the drab winter months.

Our Unruly Garden
The arrival of Spring also meant gardening chores were on the horizon. Our garden was extremely large, workmanlike rather than pretty, and with few flowers. Much of the back was taken over by the chickens, as they needed room to scratch and dig in summer, when a dust-bath kept them clean and free from parasites.

Next to the hen run was the vegetable garden, which was mainly my brother, Robert's domain, as it was important he acquired gardening knowledge for the years ahead. At the side of the bungalow stood the garden shed. It housed the gardening tools and a huge trunk, which was full of memorabilia and cups and trophies for prize-winning piggies from my grandfather's era. Now they seemed lonely and forlorn, and with nowhere to put them, they continued to stay hidden away in the trunk.

One day a mischievous kitten climbed into this trunk and got trapped inside. Was it one of the kittens that had been born in our bedroom, I wondered? A farm cat had jumped into the wardrobe and made a nest, as the long shelves were perfect for mother and babies to hide undetected amongst the linen. We were very excited when we found the new family, but kept quiet and didn't let Father know. It was lovely to watch as the kittens started to grow. But alas, our secret was not to last, as eventually, they were discovered and dispatched to the shed outside. That is where farm cats live – to keep the mice under control.

Once the kittens had been banished outside, we didn't mind being in the garden, even though weeding wasn't as pleasant as watching kittens play. Nevertheless, if we wanted pocket money, then we had to do our jobs. The front garden had bright orange marigolds during most of the summer months, and there were hundreds of them.

To relieve our boredom from the tedious chore of gardening, we often made necklaces and garlands with the daises that grew amongst the long grass in our lawn. This was more like a field – long and prickly, not mowed and manicured like the Captain's garden. His house was beautiful and his lawns were like Wilton carpet. So soft and smooth, we just wanted to roll all over them, which we could only do when he was away. He had a high society lifestyle, with exotic holidays and socializing and hunting, and all the other things posh people do. It was a source of envy for us, as we didn't have holidays away, other than to stay with relatives.

Even though the Captain had a special gardener, we could still earn extra money by doing jobs that were much too lowly for him – like picking the dandelions from his manicured lawns that dared to poke up their tiny yellow heads. We also collected petals from the beautiful perfumed roses as they were about to drop. Baskets filled with rose petals were then put into the bedrooms of the Captain's lovely house. With such a delicate aroma, the guests would be very impressed.

The river running alongside the lawns in the Captain's back garden was clear and pure and beautiful. We spent many happy moments being entertained by the ducks as they swam up and down. Then in the springtime they built their nests along the bank. I adored duck eggs, so rich and tasty and scrumptious. So we often went in search of newly-laid eggs. We had to be vigilant though, and take them whilst Mrs Duck was away, and not take too many, as she might become anxious.

Those that escaped our tea time treat hatched into little balls of fluff, bobbing about like ping-pong balls on the fast flowing water, their tiny legs paddling furiously to keep up with Mum and Dad.

After the novelty of watching their antics wore off, we went in search of other things to do on the farm. Meanwhile, to go with our teatime duck eggs, Mum had baked a cake. It was an everyday event in our house, as tea wouldn't be tea if we didn't have cake for afters. We often helped Mum with the cooking; she taught us how to weigh the ingredients by using different sizes of spoon: there were no scales or fancy equipment or recipe books for us – we knew exactly what to do. Afterwards there was always a squabble over whose turn it was to lick the scraps from the bowl. Sometimes it was too late, as the bowl had been whisked away and washed before we knew it.

Even though Mum taught us how to cook, we also had domestic science lessons at school, as having a career was not considered important for a girl in the 1950s. Cooking, darning and mending and sewing were deemed the necessary skills to be a good wife.

Deportment was also considered important and to ensure we walked gracefully and to improve our posture, we practised walking with a book balanced on our head, thus, encouraging us to 'walk tall.' And of course, not forgetting one hundred strokes of the hairbrush every morning; this was considered essential to ensure our hair was healthy and shiny. Not that it seemed to make any difference to my mousey brown hair.

Another requirement was our weekly dose of cod liver oil and malt extract, this being a government initiative during and after the war to keep the children fit and healthy. With rationing not ending until 1954, we, being farm-raised children, probably had a greater choice of food than children from the towns and cities.

However, it wasn't only vitamins and good food that kept us fighting fit; exercise was essential too. In the early 1950s there was a famous tennis player called Little Mo, and we wanted to be famous like her. 'Practice makes perfect', we were frequently told. Despite there being tennis courts on the estate, we only used them for collecting the wild horseradish that grew in abundance around the edges.

Instead, the horsebox garage worked a treat, as, having very tall doors; it was perfect for practising our strokes. In the past our continual thud-thud next door to *Top Landing's* stable door gave him a bit of a fright. Once he'd been the Captain's favourite racehorse, but when he stopped winning, they sent him to heaven; which I thought was a horrid thing to do.

Angela was much better at tennis than me. I didn't realise, until many years later, that the reason I wasn't any good at this sport was because I was short-sighted and therefore, couldn't see the ball until it arrived. This of course was much too late. Damn, I've missed it again!

When we were not playing tennis, friends sometimes came over from the town. MaryAnn had a new friend who lived on the council estate, but this friendship was frowned upon. Everything was done to dissuade the association, but they needn't have worried, as it faded away naturally and without pressure from anyone else.

Nevertheless, we didn't need friends to visit, as there were plenty of things to keep us entertained. For those times when we desperate for ideas, 'catch the apple' was a game involving a tub of water and apples floating on the surface. With a fear of putting my face under water, I found trying to catch an apple in my mouth much easier said than done. Consequently, I didn't mind when it was rainy and cold, as then we could stay inside and make paper mache objects, instead.

Sometimes, during the long sunny summer holidays, we did nothing other than lie back on the grass and watch the clouds racing across the lovely blue skies. There were also little aeroplanes flying round and round, their engines softly droning and sounding quite beautiful. The young pilots had come from the Royal Air Force training camp, not far away at South Cerney, and were learning how to do circuits and bumps. What I did not know as I lay watching those little planes, was that the man I would ultimately marry, who, being twelve years older than me, was flying one of those little aeroplanes over our house.

Eventually, bored of watching aeroplanes, I asked Mum if she wanted any errands doing. Needing some provisions from Fawkes's grocery store in the town, I volunteered. There were several different routes, but on this occasion I nipped over the wooden bridge that crossed the river and through fields belonging to Slads Farm. We often used the route to get to school, although, being a mile or so, it was quite a long way for a ten-year-old.

Not wasting time, I ran along the footpath which brought me out opposite the hospital that had been built by way of a gift of land from the Estcourt estate in 1869. Walking a little further, I peered over the quarry wall as I passed by, if only to see if the men were at work. I did this quite often when returning from school, as it was a pleasant distraction after a long and tedious day.

I also checked the railway station, but clearly there were no trains in at that moment in time, as I couldn't see the usual clouds of billowing smoke. I loved steam trains and would have been happy to camp out on the platform, if only to watch their comings and goings. Frequently, we travelled on the train to the swimming baths in Cirencester; it was a wonderful experience and an easy mode of transport, without hassle or inconvenience.

Continuing past the station, I thought I'd better not linger and quickened my pace until I reached the town centre. Upon arriving at Fawkes's shop, I gave them the list. Then I thought to myself, I could do with an apple, so I asked for a dozen apples. 'Are you sure?' the shopkeeper said, 'Do you mean a pound?' 'No,' said I, 'I want a dozen.' So obligingly they were placed into a brown paper bag and it was all put on the tab, so payment would not be made for another week or two.

On the way home I realised I had done wrong, and I thought, what am I going to do now? I'd better eat them, I suppose. Making my way back across the fields, I munched through as many apples as I could. Taking a mouthful out of one and then throwing it away and then starting on the next one, until they were all gone. When I eventually arrived home, they were having lunch and worried that I had been gone for so long. 'It's okay,' I said, 'there was a long queue in the shop.' Then I sat down without any fuss.

It didn't take me long to realise that I would suffer for my sins, and for many weeks I lived in fear, as I knew Mum would be going into Tetbury to pay her bills. Consequently, it was no surprise that upon returning from school some weeks later, she was in a terrible rage! 'How dare you!' she screamed at me, 'You are so selfish and that was a bad thing to do!' She gave me a good spanking and sent me to bed, and made me mend sheets as punishment for my crime.

Chapter Five - Nobody Told Us Why

I was about ten years old when things started to get really unsettled at home, and it was obvious there were problems, particularly, after a furious row broke out late one evening. Terrified, I hid under the bed covers! I knew it was serious, when Mum slept in our bedroom that night. We were not told anything though, as children were 'seen and not heard' and family matters were never discussed.

Arriving home from school a few days later, the house seemed unusually quiet. I couldn't hear Mum's singing or the giggles of my two little sisters. I rushed round to find them, but they were not there. Mum's clothes and my sisters' toys had gone too. But even worse was to come! Not only had Mum and my sisters gone away – Dolly, my precious 'little princess' with her pretty blonde curls and pale

Me holding Dolly

green dress and bonnet, was nowhere to be found. I was heartbroken! Dolly had been my constant companion for many years, and was the only possession that was truly my own. As I hid my tears, I knew I had to get on without her, as she wasn't coming back. But I would never forget her, and now there was only a photograph to show that she had once belonged to me.

Father didn't discuss Mum's departure, other than to say they had 'gone away.' Neither did he give a reason as to why they'd left. A few days later he gave me a letter addressed to the head teacher of Sophia's school, but I wanted to know what he had written, so I opened it. But disaster! Because I couldn't reseal it, I couldn't give it to the teacher and then I had an even bigger problem.

I suffered the penalty some weeks later, when the teachers questioned me relentlessly as to why Sophia was not at school. I told them Mum had gone to look after another family. 'Why?' they repeated. Dad hadn't given any clues in his letter to the school, so I couldn't tell them why, because I did not know.

There are many possible reasons for the breakdown of a marriage, but divorce in the 1950s was not a common occurrence, and I felt ashamed and embarrassed and would not discuss it with anyone. And as for the few friends I had, I pretended I had a mum at home and talked about her as if she was still there.

I'd always been a happy, mischievous child, but now I was suffering from a broken heart. Because nobody told me why this devastating parting had taken place, I lived with the guilt for twenty years and more. All the time, continuing to believe that the reason for Mum's departure - particularly, after the apple incident, was because I'd been naughty.

Meanwhile MaryAnn took over as mum, and even though she was only about fourteen years old, she was very efficient. And because we had always shared the household chores, we knew how to cook and clean and look after ourselves. But that did not stop me from missing Mum – the hurt and pain continued on an almost daily basis.

We had our dad, of course, but a farmer's work is never done, and he was always busy and preoccupied – and now alone once more.

And since nothing was ever discussed, we could never judge the level of pain he was going through. In spite of the change to our lives, the Sunday routine continued: church in the morning, lunch at one o'clock, and then afterwards, Dad had his forty winks. Awaking abruptly, he had a quick cup of tea, and then went back to work.

To make sure we didn't disturb Dad whilst he was enjoying his nap, we read our books. This had been encouraged from an early age, but I loved to read anyway, so I didn't need too much persuasion. Getting through two or three books every week and also *School Friend*, a magazine especially for girls. Father usually read the morning newspaper, and also *Farmer's Weekly*. He also listened to the radio, particularly *The Archers*, which was broadcast every weekday evening whilst he was having supper.

Nevertheless, even more exciting technology was on its way: television. The first time we watched TV was on the day of Princess Elizabeth's coronation. It was June 2nd 1953 – I was nine years old and somewhat bewildered by the hysteria. The problem was, there were so many adults and children squeezed into the village hall to watch the tiny television screen that I had difficulty trying to see what was going on. There again, I wasn't too bothered. After all, a sea of legs was of greater interest to me than the school desk, so I was prepared to put up with the discomfort, if it meant having the day off school.

Because of this appetizer, we were overjoyed when about a year later Dad bought our first television. I suppose it was to make up for Mum's departure, and to help us get over the ordeal. The screen was set into a brown Bakelite cabinet, and the black and white picture was incredibly small, although as far as we were concerned, the size didn't matter. To us it was a wonderful new gadget, and we could easily have become addicted if given the opportunity.

But there was no chance of that! Programmes were strictly rationed, as we were only allowed to watch it on Sundays, and then after tea. Even so, it was much better watching television than listening to the radio. With special programmes and films for children, it was the highlight of our week. Black Beauty and Lassie were my favourites; even though at times they were sad and made me cry.

50

Schooldays

I suppose it was because of my unrest at school that I didn't do very well with my studies. Apart from nature walks which I loved, and that was probably because the lessons were often around the lanes adjoining our farm. There again, Mum had taught us all about flora and fauna, so this is one subject in which I excelled.

Learning my ten times table and reading wasn't a problem either; it was all those other complicated things, like algebra and history, where I needed some help. Then after Mum went away I couldn't concentrate, as I had too many other things to worry about, so when sitting my eleven plus exam, it was pretty much a foregone conclusion that I wouldn't be going to the grammar school alongside my sister Angela.

Sir William Romney's School was more or less in the centre of Tetbury, with the main grammar school fronting onto Long Street. It was a fine old building, and where Angela spent many of her schooldays. The secondary school, where Robert, MaryAnn and I studied, shared the same name, and also the grounds, which were massive. Our school buildings were fairly new, not old and historic like the grammar school. There were about three hundred pupils, with an almost fifty/fifty split between the grammar and secondary modern.

Beautifully mown lawns and enormous old trees made it an impressive place, and a huge weeping willow provided suitable cover for the older ones having a quick snog when they thought no one was looking. At the onset of summer the tennis courts were erected and marked out by the grounds-man, but they were wasted on me, as I was never any good at this particular sport.

I was in the Oldham team, and at the end of term, we had to participate in the annual sports day. There were no excuses; everyone had to take part. The nearest I got to winning a medal was in the hurdle race. Even though I was well behind second or even third, at least not coming in last was a bit of a triumph.

Sport was part of everyday life throughout my schooldays, including hockey, which I detested. But that didn't stop me from going on a school trip to Wembley to watch an international hockey match, although in reality, I only went along for the journey on the steam train, as that far outweighed everything else.

Back at school, our lovely sports field was also used for lounging around in the summer months, in addition to other activities, such as when a big fight broke out between two of the senior girls. A huge group of children encircled the girls, jeering and heckling and encouraging them, until a teacher arrived to disperse the crowd. Detention and one hundred lines was handed out to the pair of errant girls; a just punishment for their aggressive behaviour.

In the short term, this lunchtime entertainment took my mind off problems at home, as constant anxiety after Mum's departure had stopped me from focusing on my studies. Instead, my energies were spent on trying to make sense of what was happening in my world.

But it was worth going to school for the dinners. I suppose it was because we now did the cooking at home that I loved school dinners so much. It didn't matter what they served up, it was all good. Especially the puddings: spotted dick, jam roly-poly, semolina. I loved them all.

With the school having a lot of land, some of it was used to teach the boys how to grow vegetables; these were then used in the canteen for our lunchtime meals. So whilst they did gardening and carpentry, we girls had domestic science and needlework lessons. Before my first cookery lesson, I had to make an apron to wear during lessons. Then a year later I made my summer school dress, and although not as smart as a shop bought one, it was good enough for me. Meanwhile, MaryAnn had smocked a beautiful baby dress for Louise, but I never progressed to doing such fine needlework, as that was for the really advanced. The ability to have these skills and being able to make clothes was considered essential and part of a girl's education.

Nevertheless, my needlework teacher was a difficult lady – well, as a twelve-year-old, that's how it appeared to me. When in class one day, she asked me to lift up my dress - to measure my waist, I suppose. Not wishing to show 'my privacy' for all to see, I was extremely indignant and refused her request. She was extremely angry at such insubordinate ways, and sent me to the Head for a caning for being so rude.

The punishment for my crime was meted out after assembly next morning. Humiliated and embarrassed, I lined up in front of everyone to await my punishment, whereby, a quick rap over the knuckles and one hundred lines was a good enough deterrent against the thought of any future misdemeanour. Though I reckoned, a visit to the school dentist was probably far worse, as without an injection to inhibit the pain, it seemed like savagery to me. And of course, the fearsome school nurse regularly inspected our hair for nits.

After this humiliating experience, I became reasonably well-behaved, apart from the odd occasion when I was dispatched to the cloakroom. Then one day I committed another crime! Whilst standing staring at the wall to serve my sentence, I took the opportunity to riffle through other children's raincoat pockets in order to find a sweet, or even, the odd penny. The guilt has never gone away!

Outdoor Children
School was only part of our lives, as being country kids we loved outdoor life - whatever the weather. When stuck for ideas, we were reminded of the old saying 'You never know what you can do until you have tried', so we mainly entertained ourselves. Climbing tall trees was one of our pleasures. We were not afraid, even after MaryAnn climbed the oak tree above the garage and fell through the asbestos roof. And a good job too, that Dad's car wasn't underneath, as a large dent in the roof wouldn't have gone down to well. Luckier still, MaryAnn didn't suffer any broken bones.

When not climbing trees, we had freedom of the park that had been created by Thomas Estcourt in the 16th century. It was like our own gigantic wilderness just waiting to be explored, and a great privilege to have had such beautiful surroundings right outside our own front door.

Prior to Mum's departure, we often went in search of fresh watercress for our summer salads, which grew in abundance in the clear running stream. After a quick run across the fields, upon reaching our destination, with plimsolls off and skirt tucked into knickers, we paddled into the lovely cool water, which was oh so refreshing on a hot day.

Without a care in the world, we filled our baskets full of fun and pleasure – and watercress too – before making our way home. Whereupon, we were greeted with 'Where have you been?' Time had stood still as we collected our bounty, and Mum was merely inquisitive as to what had taken us so long.

Other times, we ventured outside the boundary of Grange Farm and into the surrounding park, but with so many beautiful places to visit it was often difficult to choose; although a favourite walk was through the woods and along the banks of the River Avon. The river passed through Shipton Wood and into the lake that had been created by the Estcourt family in the late 18th century.

Before entering into the woods we passed over a cattle grid next to an old house. I was fascinated by this ancient place. Maybe it had once been a gatehouse and someone's beautiful home? Now it was unloved, forgotten and full of neglect. The gardens, along with the overgrown trees and shrubs, showed signs of past glory, whilst the broken garden gate made such an eerie sound as it swung forlornly in the breeze.

Perhaps it was an old wives' tale, but legend had it that an evil old woman lived there. So we scurried past as fast as we could. We never saw her of course, although we often pondered as to what she might look like, but our imagination was enough for us to take fright. Most definitely, we decided, she would be wearing a long, black frock down to the ground, her wispy grey hair would be tied into a bun, and she would wave her stick in the air and shout furiously at anyone who dared pass by. Unsurprisingly, we didn't hang around long enough to find out if there was any truth in the myth.

Once we were in the woods, she was forgotten. With such beauty all around, we didn't need to dwell on the likes of a mysterious old lady. Snowdrops grew in winter, and in springtime the woodland was carpeted by primroses, and a little later, by bluebells. There was so much splendour, but we couldn't take it with us, so they became memories to retrieve in later life.

During the summer months the lake was covered with water lilies and dragonflies busily flitting from place to place. There was also a man-made island especially for the ducks and wildlife, without fear of Sly Fox coming along to gobble them up.

The lake then headed off in the direction of the waterfall, at which point it tumbled and cascaded to the ledge below. When the water wasn't too deep, we often stood under the falls soaking up the cool spray upon our face; the fine mist pure luxury, as it cooled us down ready for our onward journey.

Then as the river continued downstream, it passed through meadows that were bursting with buttercups, clover, and wild flowers, whilst honey bees danced and frolicked around making best use of the sweet nectar and heavenly aroma. Then after Mum left home my life was often blighted with sadness, which spoiled these precious moments.

With such magnificent surroundings on our doorstep, we didn't need to go away for holidays; although in reality, there was little chance of that, as usually, the nearest we got to a vacation was to stay with an aunt and uncle at their farm near Banbury in Oxfordshire. Even then, we had to help with the daily chores.

It was a poultry farm, and despite being little more than ten years old when I was taught how to pluck and draw a chicken, it was a skill that a country child was expected to know. On the other hand, trips out in the old Land Rover made up for some of the hard work, and with six or more of us squeezed onto bench seats in the back, it was great fun waving to everyone as we passed by.

We got on well with our four female cousins, although two of them were older than me, and being boarding school girls, were outgoing and confident. They were extrovert, whilst I was the opposite – shy and reserved. All the same, it was such a shock when the second eldest, if she couldn't get her own way, lay on the floor screaming and kicking her legs in the air. If we had done such a thing we would have received a slap on the bottom and been sent to bed for the day.

I liked my aunt's house though, and particularly the large plate rack in the kitchen. We didn't have one of those at home and instead dried the dishes immediately they were washed, but I rather liked the idea of drip-dried plates, as it alleviated yet another chore.

Their large dining room had a table that was so enormous there was plenty of space for their family and ours too. In addition, I loved the silver condiment set, which had pride of place in the centre of the table. They also had a posh sitting room with two plush sofas. Given the opportunity I could have spread out after lunch and had a quick afternoon snooze.

If only! Except it was highly unlikely my cousins would allow me such a luxury, as there was always something happening on the farm – usually working activities – not the enjoyable variety. But it didn't do us any harm; at least we could go home, whereas my cousins were stuck with their chicken plucking.

After our stay with my aunt and uncle, I appreciated the more leisurely jobs Dad found for us, as anything was better than drawing the innards from a chicken. And in spite of our daily tasks it wasn't all work and no play, as we had fun times too. More than anything else we loved going on long cycle rides, even though our bicycles were jolly old. But as long as we didn't go out without a puncture repair kit, it didn't matter what they looked like. Mum also loved it, as it gave her a break and without fast-moving cars to knock us off our bikes, she didn't need to worry for our safety.

We always took a picnic – hard-boiled eggs, jam sandwiches and a bottle of Tizer. Then with great excitement and expectation, we started our journey. Our trips took us all over the beautiful Cotswold countryside, in particular, the newly opened Wild Fowl and Wetlands centre at Slimbridge being one of our many adventures. These were carefree, happy times; leaving lasting memories to pluck from within whenever our thoughts take us back to childhood days.

I was about twelve years old when I first became aware of the boys, and it all came about during a trip to Slimbridge. We were sitting on a hill admiring the view when we were approached by some teenage lads. They were not interested in me of course, as I was a mere youngster to them. At the time a new record by the King Brothers had been released: 'A White Sports Coat and a Pink Carnation', and from then on, whenever I heard the song, it took me back to that encounter in the beautiful Cotswold countryside.

Another of our outings was when Angela, her friend Jean and I visited the market town of Malmesbury, which, being about five miles away was one of our shorter trips. In fact it was shorter than planned, as having climbed the tower of an old church for a view over the town, the curator, unaware of our presence, locked us in and went for his lunch. Unsurprisingly, we didn't let it happen again.

Robert wasn't keen on cycle rides with a bunch of girls. Instead, he preferred to spend his time working on the farm. This insured he had a reasonable level of wealth compared to us; consequently, he had lots of money to spend on a bike. Not a new one mind you, but a good second-hand one from the bicycle shop on Church Street in Tetbury. And very proud of his new bike he was too: a lovely black machine, costing four pounds, which, at the time, was nearly half a week's wage for many a man.

Then one year, I was very privileged to have been given the opportunity of participating in the maypole dancing at the May Day celebrations. All the same, it was just as well that I had to wear my school uniform for the occasion, as I didn't have any pretty frocks. My clothes tended to be hand-me-downs from my older sisters, and by the time they got to me the best years had long gone. Unless I found a bargain when visiting a jumble sale at the town hall, as a skirt or dress could often be bought for a few pence.

On the other hand, fashions didn't change that much, so generally, it wasn't a problem wearing clothes that had belonged to an older sibling. However, wearing holes in the elbows of my cardigans was something I seemed to do with great regularity, and when they became too large for darning, a leather patch was sewn over the offending hole. Eventually, having worn all my cardigans out, MaryAnn worked a miracle and made me a cardigan out of a jumper. She was such a whiz!

There again, she had achieved many of her Girl Guide craft badges and was pretty nifty with a sewing needle. However, my fondest memory of the guides had nothing to do with craft badges; it was when, following our Thursday evening meeting, we headed straight for the chip shop, with four pennies' worth of chips as our regular treat. Father didn't support chips as being a healthy option for meals, so this was a rare delicacy for us girls.

Then some months after joining the Guides, I, alongside MaryAnn and Angela, went camping. Our tents were pitched on a field owned by the private girls' school opposite to Westonbirt Arboretum. Well, it may well have been my first proper holiday, but being packed in tents with loads of girls wasn't my idea of fun and without proper toilets, a deep trench was dug by the older guides for use as a loo. Nonetheless, I found our dip in the school swimming pool much more agreeable than using a bowl of cold water and carbolic soap for my daily wash.

With my week's holiday over, I realised I had enjoyed it more than expected. Particularly, as we often had difficulty living up to Dad's high standards. He had been brought up in the Edwardian era: a time when strict discipline was the norm. And now, many years later he was bringing us up in much the same way.

There again, punishments for bad behaviour were tedious rather than severe. These included darning socks – alas a pair of socks would not be thrown away because of a hole or two. Even worse was mending worn-out sheets, which was normal practice for many a household, during and after the war, when 'make do and mend' was a motto many folk abided by, and something we children seemed to do with great regularity.

And of course, sneaking food from the pantry almost certainly had to be done undetected, as eating between meals wasn't allowed, let alone taking food that was intended for another meal. In spite of this, Robert often ransacked the pantry when no one was around. His favourites were bread and milk, or bread and dripping – tasty snacks for a growing lad, and deliciously filling too.

Then a lucky escape! MaryAnn, armed with the kitchen scissors was attempting to cut my hair; a task that was normally done when visiting our aunt in Oxfordshire, as it was one of her many talents. MaryAnn had already proved that she wouldn't make a good hairdresser, as when young, she and Angela had gloriously long hair which, when tied into plaits, was the latest trend. Until one day, she cut one of her long plaits off, and her hair ended up half long and half short - and I didn't want that to happen to me.

Then, much to my surprise, Dad gave me some money to visit the hairdresser's in the town. What had I done that caused such generosity? I thought I'd better not question his reasons, so I took his money before he changed his mind.

Never having been to the hairdresser's on my own, I found it a daunting experience. Particularly, as I wasn't sure what I was meant to ask for. Believing that my hair was about to be transformed into something girly and pretty, I left them to it. But as I watched the clumps of hair falling to the floor, I became increasingly alarmed. Too late – they cut it so short I came out looking like a boy, which was such an unflattering hairstyle for a young girl.

Not only was I dismayed with the result, I knew that I was in for a difficult time - and I was right. Upon arriving home I was teased mercilessly by my siblings. Father, however, thought the hairdresser had done a first-class job; now he wouldn't have to pay for another hair cut for a very long time, and as far as he was concerned, that was a great way of saving money.

Chapter Six - Home Grown

Apart from the chicken run, much of our garden was used for growing vegetables and soft fruits, and if it was not in season, then we went without. Also, with Guernsey cows producing lovely thick milk, Father's daily treat was a ladle of cream. He could do this of course, as he was in charge of milking the cows, but occasionally, when he was busy doing other work, Mum did the milking.

All cows on the farm had names, such as Daisy, Annie, Molly and Mary, and we knew the names of every one. Sometimes I helped Father bring them into the milking parlour. They were always happy to come in from the field, knowing they were having something special to eat. Cow cake was their daily treat: it is made of cereal and other goodies and a tasty morsel if you are a cow, and even for a young girl – because I tasted one too, and it didn't do me any harm. I also knew how to do the milking - by hand and with the machine. My reward was a drink of lovely warm milk, as there is nothing nicer than when it was beautifully fresh and before it went through the cooling machine.

With Dad having a half pint of cream every day, there was plenty for our porridge and enough for his cup of tea, because he reckoned it enhanced the flavour. Perhaps, it also had something to do with the quality of the tea, as having purchased many varieties from London tea merchants; he then blended them to suit his own taste. My father was a bit of a connoisseur when it came to a flavoursome cup of tea. A china teapot and a nice cup and saucer were considered essential, and the tea had to be left to brew for at least two minutes before serving.

Not only was our porridge made with Guernsey milk, we also had a thick dollop of cream and golden syrup on top. Though someone always had to stir the porridge, as leaving Mum with a burnt pan was a cardinal sin. Quite often we also had egg and bacon, as having a good breakfast was considered important and kept us going until lunchtime without snacks in-between.

Any left over cream was made into butter, but without special equipment, the cream was put into a large jar and shaken until it turned thick, and delicious it was too, with scones and home-made jam for afternoon tea. Apart from marrow jam, which I disliked intensely; I rather suspect there must have been a glut of marrows one year, as we seemed to have it for evermore.

Using produce from the farm and garden cut down expense and reduced the need to go shopping in the town. In spite of this, the high street was full of variety, with many different shops, alongside the butcher, baker and grocer, so it was almost certain one of them had exactly what we wanted. Furthermore, the shopkeeper knew his customers by name and always had time for a friendly chat.

Because we lived quite a few miles from the town, the butcher and baker called directly to the farm several times a week to deliver their products. Everything was nicely displayed in the van to help Mum choose, and then afterwards, a cup of tea and a chat was part of the service. The grocery list was sent to Fawkes's store in advance, with the groceries being delivered a few days later. This was not only a convenient way to shop, it was also vital for country folk; especially, for those without transport.

Following Mum's departure, Father had to do the shopping. He hated this chore, but to help him out, Angela and I went along to make sure he bought some of the things we thought were nicer than homemade or home-grown. So off we went to Cirencester on a Saturday afternoon and with much larger shops and many more items being stocked, there was plenty of choice to part Dad from his money.

If only that were possible! But for convenience, and to make life easier, he did let us indulge in things we'd not had in the past: baked beans - Heinz 57, and a rare treat for us country folk. Heinz also did puddings in lots of different flavours, so we tried them all.

We always ate together at the dining room table. Good table manners were part of our upbringing, to ensure that wherever we were in later life, we wouldn't be embarrassed because we didn't know how to behave at the table. And if we remembered, grace was said before eating, although quite often we were in too much of a hurry and without Mum to remind us, it was put off for another day.

Talking at the table was strictly banned, not a word was allowed until we had finished our meal. Then before leaving the table, saying thank you, was not only expected, but courteous too. Furthermore, as we took it in turns to do the dishwashing, if the thought of disappearing crossed our mind; we would be apprehended before trying to sneak past the kitchen sink.

But we left clean plates in our house, as we were always too hungry to leave food, and anyway, it wasn't allowed. Everything had to be eaten or we couldn't have pudding. We weren't fussy children so generally this wasn't a problem – apart from liver, which got stuck in my throat and made me choke. Unless of course, someone accidently let the dog into the house, then, as if by magic, it suddenly disappeared.

For the days when the dog didn't help me out, and when I was really struggling, Mum might let me off, until we had it all over again the week after. It was a custom: fish on Friday and liver another day. How could we be anything other than fit and healthy children?

Spring Daffodils

We lived in a bungalow on this lovely private country estate. Situated at the top of a slight hill, it had originally been built for the owner's son and was practical rather than pretty, and very much a farmer's home. Stables and the horse-box garage were at the bottom of the garden steps, and next to them, were three pretty Cotswold stone cottages where, Mr Cuff the gardener, and other farm labourers lived.

Further down the hill was the Captain's lovely house and gardens, and next to him another stable block, with the groom living in the flat above. A small bridge over the Little Avon River was the entrance to the farm, and beyond, the private drive led up to the main road. The drive was about a mile long, and because our bungalow was high up, it was possible to see cars coming down the drive. And with my parents' bedroom overlooking the front garden, it gave me a good view - all the way to the top road.

After Mum left I often sat on the windowsill at night, all alone, waiting and willing her to come home. Because nobody told me when she was coming back, I watched for lights in the dark night and listened intently for the sound of cars coming down the drive. With the gentle hum of traffic on the top road being such an unforgettable sound, it has stayed with me for all time. But the only car I wanted to hear was Mum's. Then when the roads became silent, I knew she wouldn't be coming home that night.

Watching the daffodils gently wafting in the breeze was a comforting sight, and high above the stars looked radiant as they twinkled in the night sky. Whilst the clouds threw shadows across the garden as they drifted in front of the moon. It was such a beautiful sight, but it only deepened my sense of loss and sadness and once more, I went to bed forlorn and despondent.

Because my younger sisters had always been in bed before me, it didn't seem so bad that I had to be in bed by seven o'clock. Now I was over ten years old, I protested profusely about going to bed so early; but no one listened. Dad had his rules and regulations, and bedtimes were strictly adhered to, but it didn't seem fair that my big sisters could stay up so much later than me. Particularly, in the summer months when I could hear them outside, playing and having a good time.

Dad insisted I had my Ovaltine before bedtime, but I only drank it because of a children's programme that was broadcast on Radio Luxembourg every Sunday. And, having joined the 'League of Ovaltineys,' I received a free membership badge. At the time, we collected anything and everything, including golliwog brooches from the Robinson's jam and marmalade jars. With hindsight, perhaps we should have kept our trinkets and memorabilia, instead of throwing them in the bin.

Following Mum's departure, MaryAnn and Angela, who were in their early teens, had interests that I was not privy to. Even though I was not told me what they were doing, I knew they were getting up to naughty things, as having witnessed strange activities, I was sworn to secrecy. Father, being a farmer, tended to go to bed early, and it was then that they sneaked out of the bedroom window which, being a bungalow, was easy to do.

By listening in to conversations I became aware they were meeting another girl, but they wouldn't let me know who else they were seeing - or what they did. But it seemed like they were having moonlight feasts, as I'd seen them take food from the pantry - an activity that was strictly forbidden. Then past midnight they sneaked back to bed. Everyone was asleep, and they were never found out. They did this quite often, and I always kept their secrets.

Perhaps, I should have made life difficult for them and done and apple-pie bed, as folding the sheet back over itself would make it impossible to get into bed. I knew how it was done, as from an early age we had been taught how to make our own beds. Bed-making was quite an art, as the sheets and hospital corners always had to be neatly folded at the appropriate place.

We often played practical jokes on each other, as it was all part of the growing up process. But I think their pranks had gone too far when one day, to my horror, I found a slug buried in my salad. I leapt from the table screaming and ran around frantically. My siblings thought it was a huge joke and were laughing hysterically. Needless to say, I never forgave them as it was a horrible thing to do.

However, with school holidays on the horizon, I had other things to take my mind off this unpleasant incident, as throughout the summer months we often went swimming at the open-air baths in Cirencester. Regardless of having lessons at school, I still found the art of swimming elusive, but I was prepared to put up with that as my biggest thrill was the train journey.

I loved steam trains and would have ridden on them all day long if given the opportunity. By leaning out of the window, I could watch the plumes of smoke billowing from the chimney and breathe in the sweet smell as it drifted past my window. But most of all, it was the sound of the gigantic wheels as they covered the track and the chuff, chuff of the engine that captivated me.

We also went to see Mum in Somerset and loved our holidays with her, as there were other children all about our own age. On my first visit, my biggest achievement was learning to swim in the lido at Weston-Super-Mare, with the seawater helping me to stay afloat. At last, after months of trying I had mastered this skill.

Except my excitement was ruined, when I saw Mum kissing the father of the children she had gone to look after. Apart from the mistletoe incident, I had never seen her kiss anyone other than my father and it was a terrible shock. However, she laughed it off and said, 'I've got something special for tea.'

Mum was an expert when it came to her culinary skills. One of her greatest talents was making clotted cream, as a plateful served with homemade jam and scones was the ultimate teatime treat, and, an everyday occurrence for this family.

Nonetheless, our holiday didn't last long enough, and all too soon Dad was standing on the doorstep, ready to take us home. Angela and I weren't happy, but she made such a fuss she was allowed to stay longer, whilst I went home alone. Sad and confused, and still unable to understand why Mum left, my unhappiness seemed to go on forever, and it seemed to confirm that she had left because of me.

Throughout my childhood, our holidays were always to stay with relatives, but it wasn't a problem, because we also went on day trips to places of interest, such as Wookey Hole and Cheddar Gorge. With free parking and costing very little, it was right up Dad's street, as he never liked paying too much for anything. But before Mum departed, someone always had to stay at home, as six children and two adults wouldn't fit into Dad's car.

Then after the twins left home, Angela and I often went out with Dad for the day. In particular, I loved our trips to Lundy Island on the paddle steamer boats. The clouds of smoke billowing from the giant funnels fascinated me. And although I don't like water that much, I loved watching the big paddles as they swished round and round with unrelenting vigour, forcing the ocean to froth and bubble its way to the stern. Better hang on to your sandwich though, as those noisy seagulls would have it if given a chance.

But there was a downside to my happiness: singing competitions. My singing has always been out of tune, so I couldn't understand why Dad wanted to show me off for others to see. With no way of escaping as he pushed me into the throng of young songsters, I just wanted to get it over and done with as quickly as possible.

Ruling the Roost
Before MaryAnn started work, she ruled the roost when it came to household chores, organising them with military precision. We were designated various jobs and had to do them come what may, which didn't go down too well with Angela and me.

Even though the house probably wasn't as clean as it could have been, we were too young to worry about things like that. Better still, was the solution Angela and I found for cleaning the long hallway. To keep the surface well-polished we came up with the idea of putting dusters on our feet and then sliding up and down until we could see our faces in it, after which, a rug was placed on top. A lot of effort went into perfecting this skill, and we couldn't wait for Dad's approval when he returned for afternoon tea. But disaster – as he put his foot on the rug, the floor underneath was so shiny that he skidded and fell on the hard surface with a hell of a whack. He told us what he thought of our great work, and it wasn't exactly complimentary.

In spite of this, keeping the place clean and tidy was all very well, but anything without a home was shoved into a drawer in the sideboard, or indeed, any drawer we could find in which to hide away all those surplus items. When an item got lost we knew it would be somewhere around and almost certainly in a drawer. But which one? It was a guess, so all the contents had to be tipped out onto the floor.

Harvest Time
On the other hand, we spent as little time as possible doing housework, preferring to find more exciting ways of spending our time. Being farm children we got involved with whatever was happening at the time, as we were always keen to earn extra money. Harvest time during our summer holidays was particularly exciting, as whilst the threshing machine spent all day throwing out sheaves of straw, we children followed behind and stooked them, ready to dry.

It was hot, dusty and thirsty work, but Captain Smith-Bingham looked after his men, and flasks of cider were available to quench their thirst, and, with plenty left over at the end of the day, we children had a quick sup from the casks as we rode on top of the hayrick on its final trek to the barn.

With the harvesting over, gathering rosehips was another means of earning money. Normally citrus fruits came from far off places, except during and after the Second World War, when they were not available, picking rosehips helped provide the fruit to make vitamin

C syrup for babies and people in need. At the end of summer the hedgerows were full of hips that had ripened in the summer sun, and now a lovely rose red they were ready for us to pick. But why did the best ones always have to be at the top of the bush?

Some children in other parts of the country had time off school for rosehip picking, but we were not as fortunate and had to make do with weekends and after school. It was a mad scramble - gobbling tea down as fast as we could and then rushing to the best places. Then, having filled our baskets to the top, we took them to school next day and were paid according to the weight. These additional earnings enabled me to buy sweets and magazines and things Dad would never dream of buying, like sherbet lemons and sherbet fountains.

But it wasn't all work and no play, as throughout our time at Estcourt Park, we continued to have the freedom to roam all over the estate. And because we were fit and active, we could easily vault over a tall farm gate – which came in useful for MaryAnn, when she unwittingly walked through *Top Landing's* field. Practising his racing techniques, *Top Landing* headed straight for her. Without a second's thought MaryAnn broke into a sprint and vaulted clean over the gate. In so doing, she avoided a galloping racehorse and a potentially unpleasant situation.

With many farm animals in the fields, electric fencing was used to keep them under control and although not life threatening, passing the current down the line of several children was a game we sometimes played on unsuspecting victims. Despite our pranks, we weren't horrid all the time, and spent many happy hours with our friends and family walking and messing about in the surrounding countryside.

We also preferred cycling to school; apart from when snow lay thick on the ground. For those times we had to walk, but with the shortest route across the fields, and with enormous snowdrifts, it caused many difficulties. All the same, bad weather wasn't an excuse to take time off school. We were expected to attend, whatever the weather. And because Dad liked warmth and comfort after a long day at work, we were jolly pleased to arrive home to find a roaring fire in the sitting-room.

Chapter Seven - Leaving Home

At the age of fifteen the twins left home to start work. MaryAnn had decided she wanted to be a nursery nurse and found just the place in Stroud. I think she rather liked the idea of escaping from Angela and me, even though she had to work long hours as part of her training. Whenever possible, Father, Angela and I visited and took her out for afternoon tea. It was a popular English pastime: a pot of tea, cucumber sandwiches and homemade cakes.

Meanwhile, Robert moved to a farm near Banbury in Oxfordshire by recommendation of our aunt and uncle, and because he was a long way from home, they made sure he was well looked after. His employers had a house full of rosettes, plaques and cups to prove their expertise on a horse. There were so many, there was no chance of getting around with a sweeping brush, let alone a duster.

However, my brother preferred cows and sheep, although for some unknown reason - not pigs, despite his forefathers being world famous for their piggies. During the winter months, land on the farm was used for circus animals until the start of the next season. But Robert was a farming apprentice and had nothing to do with these visitors.

From an early age he had driven farm vehicles, so it was a foregone conclusion that upon taking his driving test at the age of seventeen, he would pass first time. And also, having been a diligent saver for many years, he didn't waste any time before buying his first car – it was a small Ford, but just the job for getting out and about.

Whilst we missed the twins, it was of great benefit to me, as very quickly I commandeered Robert's bedroom and made it mine. For many years I'd shared a bedroom and a bed with my two older sisters, and not since my stay with Aunt Win, had I a room of my own. One disadvantage, however, is that now I would have to clean my own shoes. This being a task that was normally carried out by Robert every Sunday: amidst much moaning, as he hated this chore. Nevertheless, highly polished shoes were a symbol of showing pride in one's appearance, with shoe inspection being carried our after assembly every Monday morning.

Now that I was in my early teens I had started to develop an interest in boys, in particular, Peter, a lad from school. Like me, he sat at the back of the classroom, but on the opposite side. He was extremely good-looking, so I'm sure I wasn't the only one to have a crush on him.

I'd also started to notice famous people in the weekend newspapers, and it was after Dad threw the papers out that I went through them and secreted away pictures of my favourites. One day whilst rummaging around in the garden shed I found exactly what I was looking for: an old leather suitcase. I decided it was perfect for hiding my treasure trove. So I sneaked it inside without anyone knowing and because my ancient metal-framed bed had plenty of space underneath, it was an ideal place to store the case. Not only that, since I was in charge of cleaning my own room, I knew it wouldn't be discovered by anyone else.

From then on, and whenever possible, I pulled the case out and swooned over the pictures of my gorgeous dream idols. James Dean: so young and handsome. There was also Cary Grant and James Stewart or even Dean Martin. Indeed, I would have settled for anyone young and good-looking. Oh how I yearned to be older and pretty so I could find myself a handsome young man.

But there was no chance of that whilst I was wearing my sisters' old clothes, so I reminded Father that he had promised me a new outfit. In view of the fact that throughout childhood I had continued to wear hand-me-down clothes, I was anxious to have something of my own, and it was because of this that I never forgot the only new item that I *nearly* had: a beautiful coat with a velvet collar.

When I was about eight-years-old, Mum decided we should all have something new to wear for Louise's baptism and it was after great deliberation, that three matching coats were ordered from the mail order catalogue. It took many weeks for the parcel to arrive and I was becoming anxious and getting to the stage where I couldn't sleep at night, wondering if my big day would ever come.

Eventually, a van drew up outside our house and as the back doors opened, I saw a large box. I knew then that my special moment had arrived. Being in such a hurry, I almost knocked the box from the driver's hands. He smiled wryly at me, and must have been thinking I'd never had new clothes before - and he wouldn't have been too far wrong, either.

Then I nearly took a tumble as we sped up the garden steps, but we managed to get the box onto the kitchen table without further ado. With so many knots in the string - better get the scissors out. Except Mum wouldn't let us perform such an act of vandalism, knots always had to be untied - so that we would be able to use the string again when sending parcels and presents to other people.

Inside the box, the coats were nicely wrapped in tissue paper, but already I could see they were beautiful. The fine material was in a luxurious rich blue and black herringbone design and the lining in a lovely blue taffeta. Also, with the collar and pockets being trimmed in deep blue velvet, they were certainly fit for a princess.

It was exciting for all of us, but particularly for me, as finally my wishes had come true – something new – just for me and nobody else. One by one, we took them from the box. MaryAnn's coat fitted perfectly and she was delighted. Then Angela started showing off in her new coat. Well, mine might be last out of the box, but I didn't care, I was going to be the princess I had always wanted to be. But devastation! My coat was the wrong size. My dreams were dashed. Why did it have to happen to me? I didn't want anything posh – I just wanted a new coat!

Once more I would be wearing my second-hand clothing. This was the story of my childhood days – skirts and dresses with huge hems waiting for me to grow taller, and so evident they had once belonged to someone else.

Now there was just the matter of getting to the parish church for the christening ceremony. I tried hiding behind my big sisters, so that no one would notice my clothes, as I was convinced they would know and laugh at me, 'Poor girl,' they would be saying, 'She is wearing her sister's old clothes!' Fortunately, the pews were so high nobody could see what was below chin level anyway.

With the service over, I wanted to escape as fast as possible. If I mingled with the other worshippers, they might not see what I was wearing, and once outside, I could run swiftly from sight. Then once home, all would be forgotten, as a special high tea was planned to celebrate the occasion. There was rich fruit cake, like Christmas fruit

70

cake, but a bit smaller. At least I could drown my sorrows with cake, as Mum might give me an extra-large slice to make up for not having a new coat.

After this period in my life, it was to be another four more years before my big day eventually came round. Following MaryAnn and Robert's departure, Father must have had a guilty conscience and, realising he couldn't get away with depriving me of nice clothes any longer, suggested a trip to the shops. I was approaching my thirteenth birthday when one Friday, Angela and I took the afternoon off school, and Dad drove us into Bristol.

He didn't like shopping anyway, and to be buying clothes for a young teenager was always going to be fraught with difficulties. This, however, was to be my first grown-up dress and an important milestone in my life, and I had strong views as to what I actually wanted.

Trudging round Bristol wasn't much fun for Dad, or me, and being a bit of a novice when it came to choosing clothes, I wasn't sure what I should be looking for. Consequently, it wasn't long before Dad started to get fed up, ready for a cup of tea and off back home. Then by some miracle, we came across a fabulous new style of boutique called Richards. These shops were especially for the modern teenager, and sold all manner of beautiful clothes and accessories. This really was my lucky day.

Now the hard work was about to begin. For someone who had never seen so many gorgeous clothes before, it was difficult to choose. Except my father didn't have any patience when it came to choosing clothes, and not being able to find anything fuddy-duddy and down-to-earth, he probably thought we should try another shop; in case I got carried away and found something 'too old' for my years.

But it had taken too long to find this place to turn my back on it now – so I thought I'd better put Angela to work. She was older than me and would have a better idea of what I should be looking for. So we sat Dad down in the corner, whilst we searched the rails. After a while I could see he was becoming impatient and about to prise me from the shop, when jubilation - I found exactly what I was looking for.

A beautiful dress with a scooped neckline, gathered skirt and soft green cummerbund, and I couldn't wait to try it on. Even so, as I emerged from the changing room, I could see that Dad was looked concerned and probably thinking it was too old for his 'little' girl. All the same, I wasn't backing down as I'd waited a lifetime for this special moment. Then when I saw his hand reach for his wallet, I knew that I'd won the battle.

The lady in the shop wrapped my dress in tissue paper, but it was a waste of time, as the moment I arrived home I would try it on again. Not only that, I vowed to get rid of the liberty bodice, which most girls of my generation were obliged to wear.

Come night-time and realising I couldn't wear my new dress to bed; I hung it on the wardrobe door, then I would be able to look at it all night long. Desperately I tried staying awake, as I couldn't bear to take my eyes off this stunning creation - a new dress that had been bought especially for me and nobody else.

Much to my relief it was still there next morning – I hadn't been dreaming after all. All I needed now was some new shoes to complete my outfit, but Father was careful when it came to spending money, so for those I would have to wait for another time.

Chapter Eight - Croxton Park

The atmosphere was quite different after MaryAnn and Robert left, and now, with only Angela and me at home, I believe this helped Father decide to look for pastures new. He had been through a lot of upset and turmoil over the past years, and probably wanted to leave it behind and start afresh.

Angela and I were dismayed at the prospect of moving from an area we knew and loved. But even worse, was discovering that our move would take us many miles from Tetbury to a place called Croxton Park. Situated way up north between Grantham and Melton Mowbray, it might as well have been on another planet as far as we were concerned.

Now that we were in our early teens, it wasn't easy leaving friends behind. Angela had lots of friends, whom I tended to share if given the opportunity, as being shy and reserved I had difficulty making friends. So I left behind the only friend I had. Edna, I remember her so well. Her dark, sultry looks and gorgeous black hair, which she tied into a ponytail, and long slender hands and beautiful nails; not nails like mine that were bitten down to the quick! She was tall and slim, not dumpy like me, and I envied her so much. We promised to write to each other, but it didn't continue beyond the first few letters.

Dad's new position as the farm manager for Captain Kyle had brought us, once again, to a beautiful private country estate. With its soft rolling hills and lovely scenery, we decided that perhaps it wasn't that bad after all, and although not immediately obvious to teenagers, like Angela and me, a lot of history was attached to Croxton Park. Stretching back many hundreds of years, a medieval abbey had once stood not far from our new home. The abbey was founded in about 1150, by William, the Earl of Montaigne, Parcarius de Linus, and Sir Andrew Lutterel, for the White Canons, also known as the Premonstratensians.

Not only did we have the site of an old abbey on our doorstep, the original building of our home was also old and full of character. The beautiful beams, wood panelling, picture rails and fireplaces in all the rooms, made it a special place. In addition, there were two staircases - one at each end of the house - ideal for separating the maids from the rest of the household. Not that we had maids of course, as Angela and I did the housework.

Regardless of its charm, it was much too large for the three of us. And there was another problem – having moved from a bungalow to a house twice the size, we were in need of assistance. Without hesitation an aunt came to our rescue, and being a dab hand at making curtains, before long she had transformed every room. So how much was it going to cost? 'Oh, don't worry about money,' she said, 'I'll just have that oil painting over there.' As a result, our family heirlooms continued to disappear.

At the time though, we had other things to worry about, like remembering to pump water from the well to ensure the taps didn't run dry. Also, because heating was by way of a kitchen range and log fires, maintaining a pile of wood was also essential. What's more, it didn't take long before Dad commandeered a small room in the middle of the house. This favourite place, which he kept cosy and warm, was where he read the newspaper and fell asleep without anyone knowing.

The bathroom was quite the opposite, as it was icy cold in winter, and because of this, Angela and I had our weekly bath in front of the fire in the parlour room. Nevertheless, sitting in a tin bath is not quite the place for a young girl to expose her modesty. Consequently, I was more than happy we only had a bath on Sundays, ready for clean school clothes come Monday morning.

Despite the setback with the tin bath, at least we had one very modern gadget: a telephone. To begin with, I found this new-fangled contraption somewhat perplexing and was terrified of picking the handset up. For most of the time it remained unused, as the only person to telephone was Captain Kyle, and only when he was checking up on my father, to see if he was lounging about at home. But Dad was a hard working man and didn't do such things.

Then there was the matter of school. Deep down I knew it was going to be a problem, even before our move. Compared to my previous school, this one was massive – seven hundred girls. All girls! How could Father be so cruel? This alone was far worse than

I'd expected. The only benefit I could think of was the new school uniform; at least it gave me the opportunity to have clothes bought especially for me. Except on reflection, I would have preferred another new dress, like the one Father had recently bought, but perhaps a different colour. That would have been so much better than a new gymslip and navy knickers.

Angela, being brainier than me, attended the grammar school, whilst I went next door, to the Sarson Girls High. We didn't need to get up at the crack of dawn at Tetbury, where, a fast run across the fields or a cycle ride got us to school on time. But no such luck here! Every morning we had to cycle several miles to the end of the drive and then wait for the bus that took us to Melton Mowbray.

Nevertheless, our ride on the double-decker was a novelty, as we'd never used this mode of transport at our previous home and because we sat upstairs, it gave us a good view over the lovely countryside. The buses had long bench seats, which we shared with several people, but because we didn't like others listening in to our conversation, we whispered all the way. Then upon arriving in Melton, another bus ride was required to take us to the school gates.

At the end of the day we did it all over again – except in reverse. But at least I'd managed to survive another day at a school, the likes of which I had begun to dislike intensely. Arriving back at the farm gates we had to hope that our bikes, which we had left under the hedge in the morning, were still intact and ready to ride. In past weeks there had been occasions when the cows stuck their horns under the wire and rearranged our bikes and left them with a puncture or two.

Over a period of time this new school proved to be a traumatic ordeal for me. I hated it so much, and one of the reasons was the communal showers after hockey or cross-country runs. Reaching adolescence, I was reserved about revealing my body for others to see, and I found the experience difficult and embarrassing. I had to try and think up ways of avoiding this daily nightmare. Then I came up with the idea of missing the bus. With the next one being several hours later, I would never get to school on time. But how was I going to carry out this plan? Father was fastidious about punctuality, and anyway, he didn't need an alarm clock to wake him up.

What if I changed the time on the clocks? By getting up one hour late, we would miss the bus and not be able to go to school. I gave it great thought, and after a few days decided this was definitely what I had to do. Without anyone knowing, I went round the house and reset all the clocks. This worked a treat as we all got up late. Yippee! We had missed the school bus – so one day less of torment for me.

Father was furious at my actions, but decided, as I was so unhappy, he should send me to another school. Perhaps it might not be so good academically, but it would be somewhere I could make friends and develop in my own way. All the same, I was worried about upsetting Angela, as she would have to travel alone. On the other hand, it would be better for her without my destructive behaviour, and then she would be able to concentrate on her studies without interference.

So we went in opposite directions. Settling into my new routine I was already happier riding on the school bus with other children from the village. I also had my first encounter with a lad. I remember neither his name nor face; it was the fumbled kiss that sticks in my mind. Being unsure as to what I was meant to do next, I swiftly moved to another seat before the bus filled with children from other villages. Our last stop was outside Belvoir Castle, as always, it looked very impressive and quite beautiful.

Upon arriving in Bottesford we were dropped off outside the school, and even though it was tiny, it suited me just fine. Now I was able to make friends of my own; Wendy and Brenda being my favourites, although we never stayed in touch. Apart from practising how to write neatly, I remember little of my studies.

At least with the school problem sorted, I could start enjoying our new home. The surrounding countryside was stunning, and watching the carp being fed was an interesting sight, and one I had not witnessed before. They were enormous and intelligent too, as they knew when it was suppertime. Every evening, with great punctuality they swam to the edge of the lake, their mouths open wide as they waited to be served left over bread from the Captain's house.

Angela and I often swam in the lake during the summer months, but because a young child had drowned sometime before our arrival, Captain Kyle was concerned for our safety. Quite often he and his wife were away - probably holidaying in some far-off destination, so we didn't take any notice.

Advice I should have taken notice of, as the lake was extremely deep, and because I wasn't a strong swimmer, swimming across the middle was a foolish thing to do. In the meantime, we found something a little safer, and floated around the lake on spare inner tubes we found in the garage. They belonged to the Captain's Bentley - or was it a Rolls Royce? We continued this activity for some time, and he never found out.

Upon our arrival at Croxton Park, I was about thirteen and going through a 'growing up' phase. It was also a time when walking barefoot was a trendy thing to do, and having seen the models in the magazines doing it, I decided what was good for them was good enough for me. Not only that, I had learned how to show off to the young farmhands: tempting them with my new found flirtatious ways. I was so young - what was I thinking of? Should have been concentrating on my homework!

Croxton Park: Top L/h: Water Bailiff's Cottage. Centre back: Park House Ruins. Front of pond: Stables & Captain Kyle's offices above. Top R/h: Our house

Shopping Spree

I was jolly pleased when shortly after arriving at Croxton Park, Father gave me some money to go and buy new shoes. It was the first time he had trusted me to go shopping on my own and consequently it was an exciting occasion. Finally, I could make my own choices. But as a teenager, I had completely different ideas as to what Dad actually meant when he said, 'Buy some sensible shoes.' My interpretation was something nice that I could wear with my new dress. Surely, he wouldn't want me to spoil the effect by getting anything too sensible? Or would he?

Pocketing the cash before he changed his mind, Angela and I took the bus into Grantham. After trudging round the shoe shops for hours, looking for 'sensible shoes,' it became apparent there was a huge difference between sensible and nice. Even so, I knew all along what Father had really intended: black sturdy lace-ups! These were not the type of shoe a teenager would be seen dead in, so eventually, fed-up with trying to satisfy my dad's old-fashioned ways, I found something a bit in-between, but no heavy soles, or shoelaces, and definitely not black. They were beautiful: taupe was the colour, and with 1¼ inch heels.

Very proud of my new acquisition, I rushed home to show them to Dad. He took one look and was not impressed and said, 'How are you going to wear those to school?' Nevertheless, school hadn't been uppermost on my mind when I had parted with his cash – more like my new dress. Hence, I didn't dwell for too long on Dad's foolishness in letting me loose with his money, and because there was no suggestion of going back to change them, I guess he'd decided to 'turn a blind eye.'

My greatest concern was not having anyone to confide in to discuss my teenage troubles and worries. Then Dad decided to get a housekeeper to give Angela and me a break from the household chores. Of course, it wouldn't make up for the loss of Mum, as I continued to blame myself for her departure, still believing she had left because I'd been naughty, and despite the passing of time, nobody had told me any differently.

Our new housekeeper came from foreign lands, but as Father was anti anything other than English, it is difficult to understand how he came upon this decision. All the same, we wanted her to be happy, so we tried to be extra nice to her and the children. Apart from the fact that she was very good at playing the accordion and keeping us entertained for many an hour, her sauerkraut and other culinary skills didn't particularly endear her to Father. He was more a roast beef and Yorkshire pudding type!

Ultimately, with different ideas to ours, and inflicting a strict regime, she became quite a handful. In the end, things didn't work out as planned, and she swiftly departed. So yet again Angela and I had to do all the cooking and cleaning after returning from school, instead of enjoying our teenage years.

Then a ray of sunshine came into my life – Angela and I were allowed to feed the baby animals. More than anything else I loved to make a big fuss of the calves, because like me, they were now without a mum, and I think they were very sad. To comfort them, I put my arms around their lovely soft necks and gave them a big cuddle to let them know they were not alone.

They loved to suck my fingers, rather like a baby with a dummy, and that is how they learn to drink. When I lowered my hand into a pail of milk and offered it to them, they sucked my fingers and without realising it started to drink. Hey presto! In no time at all they knew what to do. Their tongues were quite rough, like sandpaper, and very ticklish too.

In addition to the calves, the orphaned lambs were a joy, their little tails wagging as they enjoyed their bottles of milk. I loved them all, but Billy in particular. He was a special little boy lamb without a mother and I was allowed to keep him as my own.

We were best friends for a long time, Billy and me, and made each other so very happy. I couldn't wait to get home from school to find him. He loved my company and was always pleased to see me; leaping around with joy as he followed me around the farm.

One day when I was not there, he got out of his paddock and trampled and roamed all over the Captain's garden. Being fond of the roses, he nibbled them down to a stalk! The Captain was extremely annoyed when he found out, and I was ordered to keep him under control. But as Billy grew bigger and stronger, he could always find ways of escaping when no one was around.

Upon arriving home from school a few weeks later, I couldn't hear the bleating calls of my 'little boy.' Where was he I wondered? Had he escaped again? I asked my dad, 'Where is Billy?' 'He's gone to market for being a naughty boy,' said he. I thought to myself, well, perhaps he's gone to a lovely new home with some other grown up lambs. It wasn't until many years later when thinking about Billy, that I realised he had become roast lamb with mint sauce!

Without my best friend I was terribly sad. What was I going to do now? Full of despair, and with nobody to love and comfort me, I had to cope with my misery and unhappiness on my own. We didn't openly show feelings in our family, but a big cuddle would have helped me out.

In spite of Billy no longer being part of my life, there were many opportunities to earn money by doing work for the Captain and his wife. Angela earned hers by helping Cook in the Captain's lovely home, but as I was a tomboy and a bit clumsy, I wasn't allowed to handle the fine china. Instead, I was confined to feeding the chickens and collecting eggs once more. I didn't mind doing this job, as they were handsome Rhode Island Reds, and very friendly chickens. I had my favourites of course, and they always rushed over to greet me.

Croxton Park House - circa 1732

Chickens, although not like other pets, still like a bit of fuss and a cuddle, and I was happy to oblige. The only difficulty was the hen house and their run was next to the old rambling ruins of Croxton Park House. In the summer months it wasn't a problem going up there on my own, but on dark nights I was too scared to go it alone, so I bribed Angela to come with me. Sometimes, when the owls were hooting and tooting, it was very eerie indeed and no place for a young girl to be alone.

Croxton Park House was built around 1730 by the third Duke of Rutland, with materials from the ruins of the 12th century abbey. This fine mansion was used by members of the aristocracy as a hunting lodge, with the Belvoir, Quorn and Gottesmore hunts meeting there during the season. There is a legend that the Duke built this magnificent place for his mistress, but when the Duchess found out she was furious, and had it burned down.

Whatever the truth behind this story, in the 1950s when Angela and I arrived on the scene, the decay in Park House had become somewhat advanced, and it was because of this state of dilapidation, that we had been banned from going inside this once lovely Georgian manor house. But as inquisitive teenage girls, we were desperate to find out what was inside this mysterious place, and before doing so, we needed to wait until the Captain and his wife went away.

Fortunately, Dad mentioned beforehand when the Captain was leaving. So on the day of his departure, we did all our jobs before rushing up to Park House. Despite our enthusiasm, it was with trepidation that we pushed open the front door - the ancient hinges groaning and screeching as we did so. Then Angela let out a piercing shriek. A shiver ran down my spine! Was it a dead body? No! It was nothing more than an encounter with a large cobweb.

Angela became very annoyed when I laughed out loud, so I raced to the top of the magnificent old stairs. With an abundance of rooms to explore, we rushed round to find out what they had to offer and it was whilst rummaging amongst the debris that we found some old trunks and boxes. Cautiously we opened them up and to our surprise we found one of them full of love letters from a bygone era. Being teenagers, we were at an age when such things seemed unbelievably romantic, so we read them out loud.

But it was only because we didn't understand anything about passion that we found them so hilarious that we rolled around with laughter, until our sides were nearly falling apart.

Croxton Park House 2005

Finding this treasure trove had made our adventure all the more worthwhile, but before leaving these chronicles from the past, we carefully put them back the same as they had been for many years: hidden away in an old trunk.

It is fifty years and counting since this period in our lives, and although I don't remember the contents of those letters, or even who the lovers were, I feel privileged to have had the opportunity to peep inside this once grand old place. The secrets of its past remain for all time within its crumbling walls, as it stands looking forlorn, desolate and unloved and now past redemption.

A few hundred yards from Park House and the abbey site, was the house that Father, Angela and I lived in. It wasn't ancient, but it was certainly old and probably the reason I saw a ghost one night as I walked into the parlour room. There in front of me was a white shadowy figure kneeling down and saying prayers. I fled from the room screaming, 'There's a ghost, there's a ghost!'

After this terrifying experience, I wouldn't go into the room without a light, as it made me very wary. Where had this mischievous spirit come from? Was it the medieval abbey site? Or maybe, the old Park House ruins? I didn't have an answer for that.

Following this ghostly encounter, I was frightened of tending the chickens on my own in the dark, but I wanted to earn the money, so I had no choice. Fortunately, it wasn't my only way of earning money. Captain Kyle was a kindly man and offered to pay me for cleaning his offices, which I accepted readily. They were huge, covering the whole of the stable block underneath, and full of high-quality furniture. I took great pride in doing a good job and loved to polish the wood until it had a great sheen, and ten shillings was my reward. This was a great deal of money for the likes of a thirteen-year-old girl, such as me.

Whilst polishing the Captain's desk one day, he proudly showed me a new gadget: a television, which was so tiny it fitted into the palm of his hand. This was a pioneering piece of technology for 1957, and I marvelled at such wizardry, which left me wondering how they made such amazing things.

I suppose it was because Angela was less challenging and rebellious than me that one of her jobs involved working in the kitchen in the Captain's house. Because the Captain and his wife did a lot of entertaining, she often helped Cook prepare some of the wonderful meals for his visitors – aristocratic and otherwise.

One night everything was going superbly whilst the guests were being entertained, when suddenly from outside the dining room came a huge, piercing shriek: it was Angela. She had been making her way upstairs to put hot water bottles into the beds, when one of them burst. The boiling water was agonising and caused her much pain, whereupon, the guests hearing her screams rushed out to see the reason for this great commotion, and were so concerned, they sent her home to recover.

Nevertheless, such things didn't stop Angela, and it was with great resilience that she returned to work next morning, when she was asked to take breakfast up to a special guest. She opened the bedroom door and there in front of her was the beautiful Duchess of Rutland from nearby Belvoir Castle. The Duke and Duchess were regular guests of Captain Kyle, but this was the first time Angela had been asked to carry out such duties. Consequently, she felt privileged to have been of assistance to this gracious lady. Before leaving, the Duchess thanked Angela for her service and wished her a speedy recovery from the previous evening's mishap.

Chapter Nine - A Brief Encounter

With such earning potential, Angela and I had quite a lot of wealth, and now with new shoes to go with my special dress, I was eager to show them off. There again, living miles from civilisation meant that we didn't go out that often, apart from the village youth club. Even then, riding the two miles or so on bicycles wasn't exactly compatible with wearing pretty dresses. Occasionally, we went to the cinema in Grantham, as it was one of the few privileges Dad allowed us.

Despite living in a beautiful home, our rural existence made life difficult. We were too young for adult things, but also, too old for many other activities. Television wasn't considered a form of entertainment, and besides, Father had put our small black and white TV in the Snug, which was primarily his own domain. Therefore, the cinema became our first choice.

All the same, we were careful when spending our hard earned cash and the reason we chose Saturday matinees for cinema going, as this was our cheapest option. Not only that, everything was governed by the bus timetable, which at least kept Dad happy, as then he knew we wouldn't be home too late.

On a recent trip into Grantham we had seen the film, 'Love me Tender' advertised at the Odeon, and, starring my heart-throb, Elvis Presley. So we primed Dad in advance, to make sure he couldn't scupper our plans at the last minute. Quite surprisingly, he was feeling generous that day, and gave us some money to buy an ice cream. Preferring to spread the pleasure across the afternoon, we waited until the first interval before purchasing our refreshments.

With the intermission over we settled back to enjoy the remaining film. But scarcely had the lights gone down, when two lads suddenly appeared as if from nowhere and sat next to us. Then they started to chat us up. We didn't know what to do, as having led a sheltered life such behaviour was a new experience, and we became concerned by their overfriendly manner.

They were obviously emulating Elvis, as they were wearing long jackets, drainpipe trousers and brothel creepers, and their hair was brushed into a quiff. One of them was called Luke and the other Duke, although these were probably not their real names, but they fitted in with the 'Teddy Boy' image they were portraying.

At the end of the film they suggested we go rock-and-roll dancing, but considering ourselves too young to be involved with such an activity, we daren't do anything like that. And anyway, Father would be annoyed if he knew we had become involved with such 'undesirable' characters, as they were not of the traditional type a farmer's daughter would normally associate with.

Not giving up, Luke and Duke persuaded us to walk round the town instead. They obviously lived in Grantham as they knew all the street names and places of interest. Also, being a lot older, we were a little in awe of them, as they appeared much worldlier than us country girls.

It all seemed good fun for a while, but then we panicked and decided it was time we headed for home, as the last bus was quite early. But the lads were having none of it, saying, 'Oh don't worry, if you miss your bus, all you have to do is go to the police station and they will take you home.' Like idiots, we believed them, and thought – that sounds like a good idea.

Some time later, we realised that perhaps it wasn't such a good idea after all, and started to worry. Also, knowing the last bus had already departed and that Dad would become anxious if we did not arrive at the expected time - so off we went to the police station.

After explaining our predicament, we were somewhat surprised by their unsympathetic response to our problem, as we had expected some compassion for two young girls stranded miles from home.

'We can't take you home,' a sergeant told us.

'Oh dear, what are we to do now?' I cried out.

'We'd better telephone your father, so he can come and collect you,' said the sergeant.

Filled with apprehension and misgivings, I was shaking in my shoes as the policeman telephoned my father, who, being an early-to-bed and early-to-rise sort of person was about to have his cocoa, and to say the least, he wasn't very pleased.

Despite being eloquent and mild-mannered to the sergeant on the telephone, he said, 'Lock them up until tomorrow morning!' The prospect of spending the night in a police cell was terrifying, so we were very relieved when Dad eventually turned up. But it was an unpleasant journey, and upon arriving home we scurried to bed faster than ever before, as we knew we would be severely punished for our foolish and inconsiderate behaviour.

Next morning I awoke at the crack of dawn, thinking I might go and talk to the rabbits and tell them of my troubles and worries. Then as I tried sneaking out of the back door, I was apprehended before I could escape. Father was furious and consequently Angela and I were forbidden from going out. Not only that, we served penance by doing work without payment - a punishment we found excruciatingly painful, as earning pocket money had become a way of life for us.

The Hunt

Not allowed out of the house! Well, at least I found another form of entertainment, as the hunting season had begun. My father, although of fine breeding, hated snobbery, and he also hated it when the hunt met right outside our front door. On the contrary, I loved to watch the riders as they sauntered around showing off in their colourful coats, and their horses too – looking very handsome and beautifully groomed, whilst the hounds rushed and milled around, getting excited and ready to go.

Once the hunt was in full gallop, the riders didn't care where they went, and trampled all over the fields that had been carefully sown with crops for feeding the farm animals. Father was enraged by their indifference, as they didn't understand or even care about his role as a farmer. So he continued to dislike them intensely.

What's more, when the hunt wasn't chasing across the fields, we had to be careful not to upset the gamekeeper. During the spring and summer pheasant chicks were reared ready for the next season, when 'Old Grumpy' - as we called him, took great care of his investment. If we dared to encroach on his patch, then he had stern words for Angela and me, as he wasn't keen on teenage girls getting in the way and tramping through the woods; so we kept out of sight for most of the time. However, his actions meant much of the estate was out of bounds, unlike Estcourt Park, where we had freedom to roam wherever we pleased.

Then after Billy my pet lamb went away, I no longer had cause to roam the estate as I'd done before, and I believe this to be the reason Dad thought a kitten might make up for my loss. Even so, I didn't know anything about kittens, as the cats we'd had in the past had fended for themselves - just a bowl of milk a day and the scraps, and if they were still hungry, there were plenty of mice.

When my new kitten arrived, I called her Suki. She was so tiny, and I was afraid to hold her too tight in case I crushed her little body. I think she was the runt of the litter, as she remained very small, but it didn't matter to me, as once again, I had a special friend to love and cherish.

Angela and I had a large plant growing on the wall outside our bedroom window, and clever little Suki found out how to climb to the top of this plant and sneak into our room at night. Encouraging her into my bed was easy to do, and because she was silky-soft and beautifully warm I cuddled her all night long.

I tried to look after her as best I could, but nobody told me what to do. Then one day, she disappeared. I felt guilty after she had gone. Why did she go away? What had I done wrong? Had I not looked after her properly? Or had she found a new home? But one thing was for certain; no one could have loved her more than me.

Yet again, sadness took over my life. At times I was so lonely that often I went out on my own, spending hours wandering across the hills and valleys, trying to find ways to end my misery. Eventually exhausted, I had to go home. The wild rabbits, however, were suffering a fate far worse than me, with an epidemic of myxomatosis, and it was terribly sad to see these little creatures unhappy too.

Despite being good friends, Angela and I didn't talk about our grief caused by Mum's departure. I suppose it was because Dad didn't openly express feelings; that this same characteristic had passed on to us. All the same, we had lots of fun playing hide-and-seek, as living in such a large house there were plenty of places to hide. Not all of the rooms were used, as there wasn't enough furniture to put in them, but the many cupboards, nooks and crannies and big shutters, provided suitable cover to remain undetected for a very long time.

A large room at the end of the house remained a mystery to me. It was bereft of furniture; it's only adornment being a large oil painting hanging above the huge mantelpiece. And rather strangely: a massive laundry basket sitting in the middle of the room. Why was it so strategically placed? Was it from a bygone era and now no longer required? Whatever the reason, it was terrific for hiding in. So when it became my turn to hide, the obvious place was to leap into this basket and keep very quiet. I thought Angela would find me almost immediately, but that didn't happen, and with my phobia for cramped places, I jumped out again.

Finding another place wasn't a problem, as farming students often stayed in our house, and it became an excuse to go and hide upstairs: on their side of the house. However, Dad, had he known, would have condemned our actions as being an unwelcome distraction for young lads away from home and straight out of college.

Nevertheless, he was always working and the reason we loved having the company of other young people. Living in an idyllic rural retreat was all very well, but with few visitors, it was lonesome at times. Apart from helping with the lambs and calves, Angela and I

My Father, circa 1957 in front of Water Bailiff's Cottage & Captain Kyle's residence

weren't allowed to help with farming jobs as we'd done at Grange Farm. Unless, of course, Captain Kyle was away, then Dad sometimes allowed Angela to drive the tractor across the fields.

In spite of these restrictions, I enjoyed country life, and I also loved the sound of the pheasants at the end of the day. Such a joyful sound – as if they were calling to each other and saying: 'Time for bed, time for bed!'

I loved Selma too - she was Captain Kyle's beautiful brown Labrador, and a very lovable creature. She wasn't just a big softie though, having been trained as a gun dog, she loved to participate in the great shoot.

When her master was away she was looked after by Cook or the gamekeeper, but she didn't have the same fun as when Angela and I kept her entertained. Being a whiz at playing ball she outran us every time, chasing and running until exhausted, and then rolling on her back until we tickled her tummy. Even so, we had to make jolly certain we didn't knock turf out of the Captain's lawn, as it would have been nearly as bad as when Billy ate his roses down to a stalk.

It was on these same lawns that the Captain and his friends played croquet; such a leisurely existence for them, whilst everyone else was working. Nevertheless, Angela and I knew where the croquet set was stored, and when no one was around we had a quick game. But, living in fear of being discovered by the unexpected return of the Captain and his wife, we never mastered the art of playing in the way we'd seen others perform,

Despite our initial misgivings and even though we would have preferred friends close by, Angela and I had become settled in our new home. Nonetheless, we weren't prepared for change to happen so soon, as we had only been at Croxton Park for a year or so, when Dad decided he wanted a position without the same heavy workload. He also wanted company, other than that of two teenage daughters. For some time he'd been having ballroom dancing lessons in Nottingham: a passion he'd enjoyed as a young man. All the same, these late nights weren't compatible with his role as a farmer, and because of this, and also, because he'd had back problems for many years, a decision was made to move nearer to the Nottingham region.

This made me quite sad as it seemed like I'd been on the move for most of my life. Even so, I think Dad had made up his mind. However, before such time, he agreed that we would have a trial run into Nottingham one Saturday night, and then we could see what urban life was all about. Well, I knew immediately what my reaction to that would be.

But what a surprise! When we drove through the city, I changed my mind. With all the dazzling lights, department stores, cinemas and public houses, and so many people - all dressed in their best and out to have a good time. Father didn't have to say any more, he'd won me over. This new life looked so exciting, and I couldn't wait for the adventure to begin. After all, I had been a country bumpkin all my life, and now it was time for a change.

Change of Direction
Initially, we moved to Plumtree, a pretty country village a few miles from Nottingham, and where Dad took on another farming role. Not having reached the age of fifteen, I had to attend a school in West Bridgford: this was to be my last, and I couldn't wait to leave as I'd never really enjoyed school.

We had been allowed to wear whatever we pleased at my school in Bottesford, and without a uniform I was subjected to wearing Angela's cast-offs from her school in Melton. Once again, she had a new outfit, whilst I got the hand-me-downs. But it didn't really matter, as I looked so smart in my uniform and because I spoke quite posh, everyone thought I had come from a private school; which in all probability helped me to attain the privileged position of becoming a Prefect, and then, a Deputy Head Girl. This was almost certainly the greatest achievement in the whole of my schooldays, and I felt very proud, and Father even more so – apart from the fact that he had to buy me new school colours to go with my promotion. Finally, I had done something right.

He probably wouldn't have had the same opinion had he known that I was joining some of the other girls for a quick smoke during our lunch break. Just one cigarette between us – handing it around until everyone had had a quick puff. We pursued this bad habit surreptitiously and undetected for some time, even though I should have set a better example to younger pupils. In spite of this, I was enjoying my new status and determined to make the most of the little time I had left as a schoolgirl. Particularly, as it had taken my entire school life to get to this position.

Approaching my final Christmas, I was looking forward to the school bash, which I had been helping to organise. But that idea came to an abrupt end after I trod on a sewing-needle whilst Angela and I were practising our rock and roll techniques. The needle buried itself deep into my foot and I ended up in the casualty department to have it extracted. This was a huge disappointment, as someone else took my place at the head table. There was also frustration at missing the badminton finals, as it was the only sport I was really good at. And if nothing else, a little silver cup would have reminded me of my final year at school.

Even though the careers advisers had been to see us, I was still none the wiser as to what I actually wanted to do with my life. Careers for young ladies were not considered to be of great importance, as since the age of eleven we had been trained in the art of how to be a good housewife and it was expected that many would follow this pursuit, rather than to have a useful career.

What - Another Move?
We had only been at Plumtree for a short time, when we were on the move again. Father's back problems were a continuing saga, and consequently, he could no longer continue farming. This time we went to live in Mapperley, a suburb on the north-east side of Nottingham. It was a temporary place, until Dad found another job.

Soon after the move, and perhaps to make up for the upheaval, Dad treated Angela and me to posh new bicycles. They were the latest Raleigh models and in pretty colours too. In the past owning such lovely bikes would only have been in our dreams, as they were nothing like the ancient black second-hand ones we had to put up with throughout our childhood.

Desperate to show them off, we spent many hours exploring the local countryside. The problem was, we were approaching an age when we considered riding a bicycle as not the sort of thing young ladies did, and before long, the novelty wore off and our bicycles were shoved into the back of the shed.

Then one Sunday morning, fancying a bike ride, I opened the shed door, but my bike had gone. I didn't say anything to Dad, as I felt guilty for not making better use of my bicycle. Whilst he was probably thinking we were most ungrateful, as they had cost him upwards of twenty pounds each. And then, determined to teach us a lesson and to get some of his money back, I guess he sold them to a more deserving teenager.

In spite of no longer having my posh bike, I suppose it was because we had city life on the doorstep that taking the bus into Nottingham was a novelty, and more exciting than riding a bicycle. What's more, being teenagers, Angela and I, had the time to go window shopping and daydream of the time we might be able to afford the lovely clothes on offer in the stores and boutiques.

However, there was an occasion when our high jinks led us astray. But no wanton damage, mind you, that wasn't our style. Whilst walking down Westdale Lane, we noticed scaffolding leading up to a flat roof, when suddenly one of the lads grabbed a pole and scaled to the top. I looked at Angela and could see she had the same idea, so we followed pursuit. With such a huge expanse of rooftop it was ideal for practicing our dancing skills, even if a little hard on the feet. All the same, Dad would have grounded us, had he found out.

We often walked around Mapperley, and probably, right past the house of the man I would eventually marry. This young man, who was living less than a mile from us, had flown his RAF aeroplane over our house whilst we were living in the Cotswolds. Not only would he be part of my life, he would also become my inconsiderate and adulterous husband. Unbeknown to me, my destiny, my future, was only a few streets away, waiting to rear its ugly head!

Initially, I hadn't wanted to move to city life, until I saw the bright lights, then I changed my mind. Except after a while, the novelty wore off as I missed country life and the freedom to roam wherever I pleased. I longed for green open spaces stretching as far as the eye could see, and watching animals in the fields, with only the sound of the cows as they grazed in the meadows. I also missed the early morning birdsong and the pheasants late at night. Oh how I missed the peace and quiet.

However, there was no going back in time, as having nearly reached the age of fifteen; my search for work had begun. There was no shortage of jobs, but which one? This was a massive decision. Many girls went to work in a factory or an office, and for the lucky ones hairdressing was a popular choice. But my aspirations went beyond working in a shop.

Over the past couple of years, Angela and I had spent many hours messing about with our hair, so hairdressing seemed like a good idea. Nevertheless, in 1959 a bond of fifty pounds was required before serving an apprenticeship, which generally, lasted for about five years, but because my father had started his new life, I didn't want to burden him by asking for a loan.

And anyway, I felt flattered to have been offered the first job I applied for and I wasn't going to turn it down. So now the next chapter in my life was about to begin. Despite these new beginnings, I was still looking for love and happiness. Since the age of ten, I had never stopped blaming myself for Mum's departure, but it seemed no one was going ease my burden by telling me any differently.

Chapter Ten - CityLife

There were no party celebrations for me on my fifteenth birthday, as it was to be my first day at work. Not in the hairdressing job I had really wanted, but working in the offices at William Hollins on Castle Boulevard in Nottingham. The company was world famous for its Viyella brand of clothing and fabric, and a jolly good place for a young person starting out, with many opportunities for the enthusiastic worker.

Despite missing out on a birthday cake, I was excited at the prospect of receiving my first weekly pay packet; which was all of two pounds and ten shillings. It seemed such a lot of money, although out of this I had to pay Dad for my upkeep and bus fares.

My role as an errand girl included delivering mail throughout the company, as like many of my generation it took time to climb the ladder to success and promotion. On my first day, I noticed a feeling of exhaustion come mid-afternoon, but it didn't matter as I was happier having left my schooldays behind. There was just the matter of ensuring I didn't get lost on my way round the massive building.

Deciding what to wear was another problem, as apart from my school uniform, I had few clothes. But I had a plan. For some weeks, I'd been very diligent in helping with the household chores and I didn't moan when Dad asked me to make a cup of tea: apart from forgetting to brew it for two minutes. In fact, I was so nice he must have been thinking I'd got something up my sleeve. He was right of course, but I wasn't letting on. Until eventually, out of the blue, he said 'You can keep your first week's wage to buy a new dress.... but make sure it's something suitable for work.' Thanks Dad! This meant that the many hours Angela and I had spent window shopping over the past months, hadn't gone to waste.

All the same, having lived in the country all my life, I had little dress sense. Dungarees and wellington boots were more my style. But not to worry, there was a revolution going on in the high street for the younger generation, with an array of lovely skirts, denim jeans and pretty dresses, and all for the likes of Angela and me.

If only I'd been able to resolve my blushing problem I would have been happier. Maybe, living in the country throughout childhood hadn't helped, as I wasn't used to talking to unfamiliar people, and that's when the problem occurred. Then there was the issue of money, as despite being taught thriftiness as a child, there wasn't a penny in my purse by the end of the week. However, to ensure we didn't skive off early on Friday, we had to wait until late afternoon before our wage packet was hand-delivered to all employees within the company.

Then a few months after starting work, I was promoted to the Kardex addressing system. What's more, shortly after that, I was put in charge of supervising others doing the same work. If only my teacher could see me now. 'Could do better' being a common remark on many of my reports. And even though I didn't always take notice of my father, he was probably right when reminding us of the motto, 'If a job is worth doing then it's worth doing well.'

But perhaps a girl I worked alongside had the answer when she said 'You could get any job you want, as you speak like the Queen.' This was because Father hated slang and bad language and we had to speak properly, and also, when young we had to practise our vowels: 'How now brown cow', and other phrases too. We'd never been a family of gossipers though, the motto 'Gossip and idle chatter spreads lies' being a principle we abided by.

Initially, my work took me all over the building and even though making friends continued to be a problem, I was more interested in the lads than having lots of girlfriends. Discovering how to flirt was a new experience and I took advantage whenever the opportunity arose. On the other hand, it may also have been because I was still feeling the pain and guilt after Mum's departure, and the attention I received became a substitute for the love and affection I craved?

Nevertheless, my new position took precedence over my philandering ways. A little disappointing perhaps? But a price worth paying, as during the course of my work I came across many of the secretaries and realised that I too could become a secretary. Not only would I have reached the pinnacle of my career, but I would receive a four figure salary, and also, have an office of my own.

I couldn't just dream about it though, I needed to enrol at night school to learn shorthand and typing. And then, another three to four years of hard work and discipline was required before achieving my goal. On the evening of registration at my chosen college, I joined all the other young girls in the queue. But disaster! When it became my turn, I was told to come back when I was sixteen. Despite pleading with them, they refused, stating they had to abide by the age restrictions imposed by the college.

Full of despondency, Angela and I caught the bus home. Well, I may have been downhearted, but I certainly wasn't defeated and decided that I needed to think of some other way of overcoming this obstacle. So I connived with my father to help me do something about it, by persuading him to write a letter to my employer - stating how anxious I was to further my career within the company. And to my delight, this did the trick, as I managed to get typing lessons in the typing department. Needless to say, I was jolly pleased with Dad's handiwork.

The managers' offices were mainly in the front of the building overlooking Castle Boulevard. This prime position allowed them a good view of the world outside. Being the hierarchy, they didn't share the canteen with us, their morning coffee and afternoon tea was brought to them: lovely white bone china and beautifully served upon a silver tray – a privilege that went with their position. But goodness knows what they got up to behind closed doors, as to spice up their lives; they certainly had an eye for the pretty young girls.

In the office next to them was their secretary, as it was a time when men never did typing – this task was classed as a job for the girls. The manager's role involved attending meetings and afterwards, dictating at great speed to their secretary, who took notes in shorthand and then very accurately typed the correspondence.

I often daydreamed about my future secretarial role and had already planned my wardrobe. I would wear a smart white blouse and a navy blue suit, and by necessity, neat black court shoes with little heels; sharp enough to protect myself from a frisky manager, but small enough not to trip over when rushing to leave work every evening.

I wouldn't be the only one that wore smart clothing, as most office workers were well-dressed; although never frivolous or casual. Because I wasn't used to city life and dressing up, when going on my rounds to the various offices, I was fascinated by two upper-class gentlemen. They were probably only in their mid-twenties, but as far as I was concerned that was quite old, as I was still under sixteen.

Roger and Peter worked together in the same office. Roger had lovely blond curly hair and was tall and exceedingly handsome. I was smitten by his good looks and as a mere teenager, immediately fell in love. But if he wouldn't oblige, then there was Peter, who was also tall and good looking.

Not only was I in awe of them, I was intrigued by their attire. Pinstriped suits, bowler hats, and whatever the weather, long slender black umbrellas – making them look every bit the city gent. We certainly didn't see country folk dressed in this manner, and I suppose the reason that it was such a surprise, as Father in his farming days didn't dress up; unless it was market day, and then, he would be in his country tweeds.

At the end of my working day, I waited for Angela so that we could travel home together. She worked on the top floor and had longer hours than me, but to ensure I didn't miss her, I hung around underneath the clock above the main entrance. Then when a flood of girls descended upon Castle Boulevard, I knew she would be somewhere around.

Our twenty-minute morning coffee and afternoon tea breaks, made up for the long hours; and the canteen even more so, as they had wonderful snacks and all for a few pence. And because we had one and a half hours for our lunch break, we had plenty of time to go swimming or even dancing at the Locarno ballroom. These sessions were hugely popular and attended by many of the young. Rock and roll was our speciality and the highlight of our lives. Eddie Cochran, Little Richard, Ricky Nelson and Jerry Lee Lewis were some of my favourites, and later on, Angela swooned over Cliff Richard, but Elvis was the one for me.

Our dresses had full skirts and umpteen layers of petticoats and were reserved for special occasions and Saturday nights. But before such time, we needed to ensure the petticoats were stiff enough to make our skirts stand out, and the secret was to soak them in a starch or sugar solution. After which, they were drip-dried, before the laborious task of ironing the many yards of net took place.

To complete our outfits, we wore high-heeled stiletto shoes and long white gloves. Usually, we made our own dresses, as buying ready-made clothes was expensive, whereas material and patterns were much more affordable. But my impatience sometimes got the better of me when wanting to 'do it all in a day.' And Angela, who was much better at making clothes, helped me whenever I got into a muddle with the yards of material that went into the making of the voluminous skirts.

Showing off our lovely dresses was easy to do, as Saturday nights were Locarno nights, and that meant rocking-n-rolling the night away. Admission was only a few bob and a milk-shake or a glass of bitter or mild lasted the evening, so it didn't cost a fortune. Teddy Boys were also part of the scene, wearing long jackets, drainpipe trousers and brothel-creepers, and with their hair brushed into a quiff or a kiss curl, they were clearly imitating Bill Hayley.

Angela, and her friend Rita and I danced together for much of the time, in the hope of catching the eye of a handsome young lad - but all they did was stand around checking out the pretty girls before making a strike. All the same, it was no good a lad thinking he could take us over for the evening. That would only happen if he was a good dancer, otherwise we would ditch him as fast as possible.

When I was still under the age of sixteen, we came across a nice young man called Ray. He was my first boyfriend, and I was infatuated by his good looks. His lovely black wavy hair and pouting lips, made him look like Cliff Richard, but much more handsome. Especially, when wearing his trendy Black Watch tartan jacket.

Ray was a few years older than me and worked down one of the coal mines in the Nottingham region and lived with his parents in a council house. His shifts meant that he often met me from work, and being anxious to show him off to my fellow workers, we walked arm-in-arm from Castle Boulevard to the bus stop in the Old Market Square. Upon reaching Toby's department store at the bottom of Friar Lane, I gazed longingly at the wonderful displays in their windows, and for me, all manner of unaffordable things.

Ray and I went out together for several months, but one day he met me from work and told me he couldn't see me anymore. I was heartbroken! He explained that we came from different backgrounds and over time things wouldn't work out. On the contrary, I thought he was perfection and his background didn't matter, so I pleaded with him. But unlike me, he didn't wear his heart on his sleeve and when he said 'It's for the best' I didn't think he really meant it. Then, in the hope of meeting up, I went to the Locarno for weeks upon end, as I was certain I would be able to change his mind. However, the opportunity didn't come about and I never saw him again.

My misery was compounded after having yet another argument with Dad. I'd just lost my first boyfriend and he didn't seem to realise the amount of pain I was going through, but life goes on and there were other activities in which to participate, such as swimming and tennis. Angela and I had also joined the local youth club; despite having to attend the church service before meeting at the village hall. Even so, the club was good for us as we had lots of fun times.

During the summer months, our Saturdays were often spent at the open-air lidos scattered around the Nottingham area. All day swimming and sunbathing and having a good time, and it goes without saying – chatting up the lads and planning our Saturday night out. I remember wearing my first bikini at the Carrington lido. It was so pretty: a mottled green with frills around the top. I kept it for many years, as it reminded me of my youthful days and some of the good times.

Come Monday morning, Angela and I had to get to work on time and because of these long hours, we rarely went out during the week. Apart from summertime: when we might hang around the street corners for a while; this having become a popular pastime for the young.

Whilst walking back home one day, we were encouraged to have a cigarette by some of the other guys. Apart from a quick puff when I was at school, this isn't something I'd taken up. So when they said 'Put it between your lips and in inhale deeply' I did as instructed. Momentarily it felt good, but then I felt giddy and as the ground spun beneath me, I thought I was going to fall. Then when the choking started, I thought 'What a way to die!'

One would think that as my father had never smoked, I wouldn't partake in such a habit, but unfortunately, even after believing I was at death's door with my first ciggie, I hadn't learned my lesson. The following week I was encouraged to have another one, and so there began a habit that took a lifetime to break.

Well, at least I survived for long enough to enjoy another Sunday afternoon at Woodthorpe Park, but not before spending an inordinate amount of time getting ready. The bouffant hairstyle of the day had to be backcombed and teased and prodded into place, before being lavishly sprayed with copious amounts of lacquer. This ensured that a sudden gust of wind couldn't blow it out of place. Even then, before leaving home a chiffon headscarf was gently placed over our hair and surreptitiously removed at the park gates.

Dad, however, was a bit of a spoilsport by insisting we had our traditional Sunday lunch before allowing us out of the front door. This usually consisted of roast beef or chicken, with roast potatoes and Yorkshire pudding. Followed by a delicious homemade apple pie or steamed pudding with custard. There were no deviations, and it was always served at one o'clock.

It had taken years for Father to perfect the art of carving a slice of meat, which was often so thin you could almost see right through it. But at least this meant the leftover joint could be served cold on Monday and as shepherd's pie on Tuesday. And, because most folk knew how to cook, it was also a way of making food go further.

With Sunday lunch over and having done our part with the washing up, Angela and I made a dash for the back door. On windy days, we had to hold our dresses down otherwise we might show more than intended, but with the amount of wolf-whistling aimed in our direction, we knew our efforts hadn't been in vain. My wardrobe wasn't exactly stuffed full with clothes, so I had to be very cunning, and the answer was to alternate my cummerbunds and cardigans throughout the summer months. This gave the impression that I had pots of money. If only!

Upon arriving at the park, it was important to find somewhere prominent in order to view the lads as they passed by. We were especially looking for those who were in possession of the hottest new gadget: a transistor radio. Their prime role in life seemed to be to show off this wonderful new invention, whilst serenading everyone with the latest rock-and-roll music. If we sat next to them we could listen to our favourite pop-stars, and if we were lucky, we might find a handsome young man into the bargain.

Whilst lazing about watching the world go by, we had noticed that the Teddy Boys, especially, always put on quite a show. Their fabulous long jackets had velvet lapels and were in bright colours: yellows, pinks and blues, and with a peep of fluorescent ankle sock embracing thick soled brothel-creepers, they were certainly colourful characters.

It was interesting watching them as they sauntered around showing off to the crowd. Nevertheless, being conservative in my ways, I could never imagine taking a Teddy Boy home to meet my father, as I don't think he would have approved. Not that there was anything wrong with them, of course. They were just different from other young men, often hanging out in groups and being quite noisy, but it was all part of the youth culture at the time.

Sunday afternoon in the park became a highlight of our lives for several years, it was an innocent and pleasurable way of whiling away the time, whilst occasionally, pitting our wits against the boys on the crazy golf course. Then as time went by, Father decided he needed to introduce Angela and me to a more refined way of life, so we were coerced into taking up ballroom dancing lessons. Over the years he had danced his way around many ballrooms and had become an accomplished dancer, with countless medals to prove his expertise on the dance floor.

To keep him happy we decided to give it a try, if only to stop him pestering us to do something worthwhile with our lives. However, to be any good, we needed to be more enthusiastic, and that meant getting up early on a Saturday morning, when all we wanted to do was to have a lie-in for a few extra hours.

It was okay for a while, but we had difficulty trying to keep up with Dad's standards. After all, rock-and-roll was more our sort of thing, and it didn't take long before deciding that dancing shoes, layers of frothy satin and net petticoats was not our style. Father was disappointed with our lack of commitment, but nothing he said would get us back to this Saturday morning ritual.

Chapter Eleven - A New Stepmother

A few days before my sixteenth birthday, Father remarried for the third time. Initial trepidation turned into excitement with the belief that now I would have someone to make my bed. I was fed up with having to do this chore, and thought it would be great to come home from work every evening and find my bed neatly made and ready to climb into.

It seems rather silly to think this was ever going to happen, but also, that something so simple should have held such importance. Besides, my new step-mother wasn't a homemaker; having worked all her life she was a career woman with a good job, and there was no way she was going to make my bed. But that didn't stop me from wanting someone to do all those special things that mothers do best. The problem was I'd missed out from having a mum since I was ten years old, and all I really wanted was someone to take over from where she'd left off.

I'm not sure why Angela and I weren't invited to the wedding. Perhaps, Father was concerned I would behave in my normal way, which quite often, was confrontational and argumentative, and therefore, he didn't want me to be around to spoil his special day. Or more than likely, he didn't want Angela and me to have time off work, as our holiday entitlement, like the majority of workers, was only two weeks each year, and we wouldn't have been paid. We could have skived off work for the day of course, although that was highly unlikely, as Father would never condone such behaviour.

The wedding wasn't discussed in advance of the big day either. Presumably, so that we couldn't make plans or take advantage of having the house to ourselves. But I don't think Father had thought this through, as it was rather silly being on his honeymoon on my sixteenth birthday. After all, sixteen was a milestone in my life. We had to think of ways to tell Dad that a few friends were coming round to celebrate. Then we decided to wait until he was about to walk out of the door, that way, he wouldn't be able to do anything about it. Nevertheless, the idea of leaving two teenage girls in his future marital home didn't go down too well, but since he had other things to occupy his mind, he agreed with the understanding that we wouldn't annoy the neighbours.

We didn't have loads of friends anyway, and it was going to be a simple affair, but somehow word got round there was a party at our house. Being young and inexperienced in the ways of the world, it didn't occur to Angela and me that the hordes of people who descended on our house that night were in fact gate crashers. And they just kept arriving!

In no time at all we had a house full of strangers, but it got even worse. Someone went into the pantry and ate all the food that had been left for us. Then the ham that Father had been curing for many weeks was also eaten. Before long we were bereft of food and had the neighbours knocking on our front door telling us to quieten things down. Oh, boy! One thing was for certain: I would be in deep trouble when Father returned home with his new wife.

Conflicts At Home

Even without the goings-on at my party, problems and conflicts had been festering for some time, but now things were out of control, as I became even more rebellious and horrid. Angela, on the other hand, was good and placid, and witnessing my behaviour must have been difficult for her. All I wanted to do was run wild and vent my anger and frustration upon the world. I was a tormented teenager, and deeply troubled and confused.

Not only that, I was disappointed that my new step-mother had not taken over from Pamela, my first step-mum, in the way I would have liked, but I was too young and naive to understand that was never going to happen.

Pamela now lived even further away and contact ceased beyond the odd letter or card, and because her reasons for leaving our Cotswold home were never talked about, I continued to believe it was because I'd been a naughty child. Those feelings of guilt continuing into my thirties, until one day, I realised it really had not been my fault.

Despite my father's recent marriage, he still tried to show he cared, and often took Angela and me to the pictures as a special treat. The epic film Ben Hur was shown at the Odeon cinema and on another occasion, South Pacific: a particular favourite of Father's as he loved anything musical.

Janet, my new step-mother was also trying to get to know me better, perhaps in an endeavour to understand the mind of a teenager. This was always going to be difficult, as I was naturally cantankerous and felt everyone was against me, so nothing she did would make any difference. It wasn't her fault of course, but no one could take the place of Pamela, my first step-mum.

Regardless of my problems, I managed to reach the age of sixteen unscathed and when Janet offered to colour my hair, I was over the moon. Since my early teens I had wanted a more glamorous hairstyle; believing it would change my life and make me happier, and therefore, nicer to those around me. Not only that, she had bought Angela and me petticoats for Christmas. I was thrilled, as it was the prettiest garment I'd ever owned. Mine was a delicate shade of lemon and Angela's was pale blue.

Then a few months later my brother Robert suggested that a short holiday might help ease the tension that had building up at home. I thought this a wonderful idea, as it would give me the opportunity to show off my new hairstyle. Robert had recently passed his driving test and, having bought a small Ford car, was anxious to demonstrate his driving skills.

After much deliberation, we decided that a caravan holiday on the Isle of Skye would be a great adventure. We'd never been so far from home before, as all our holidays had been to stay with relatives or camping with the Girl Guides, so this was to be a special trip. But how did we all get into Robert's car? With MaryAnn, Angela and her friend Jean, and me, it must have been a hell of a squeeze.

Not only that, it was a long way from Nottingham to the Isle of Skye, so whose suggestion was it to go so far, anyway? To make sure Robert didn't buckle under the strain of the narrow winding roads of the Cumbrian Mountains, we planned our route carefully. And it was whilst travelling through the Lake District that we were taken by surprise. We had lived in some lovely countryside before, but the breathtaking scenery made us stop and take in the views. Waterfalls cascaded from mountain tops and the magnificent landscape changed colours as the sun darted in and out of the clouds. Everything around was so natural and undisturbed, with only the sheep bleating and the birds calling from above. We had found another paradise: so different from Cornwall or the Cotswolds, but such a delight.

Then with the lakes many miles behind us and after a short trip on the Glenelg to Skye ferry, our first proper holiday was on the horizon. And getting late it was too, by the time we arrived at the caravan site, whereupon, Robert, having driven almost three hundred and fifty miles, refused to be involved with any chore, other than to drive us around the island; and probably round the bend, as he could be quite a menace at times.

Extracting ourselves, and our belongings from the car, we surveyed our surroundings. But as the farmer's wife opened the caravan door, we realised why Robert had allowed us few luxuries: it was even smaller than small. Nevertheless, I insisted on taking my lipstick, mascara and stilettos just in case an occasion arose whereby I might come across a handsome young Scottish lad.

For some unknown reason Robert slept in his car that night, but there again, sharing with four girls was probably too embarrassing. We'd planned to have a lie-in next day, but the cows mooing and the cockerel crowing at four o'clock in the morning ruined that idea. Anyway, Robert was ready for his egg and bacon. Until we reminded him that we were on holiday and there was no chance of that. Settling for a bowl of cornflakes instead, we then went in search of the nearest shop to buy our groceries. Baked beans was top of my list, as having been deprived of them for much of my childhood, I was more than happy to have them for breakfast, lunch and tea.

After allowing Robert recovery time from driver fatigue, we planned a trip out. And it was whilst exploring the island, that we discovered the wild rugged landscape, pot holes, blind summits and cattle grids were all part of the experience. Not only that, we came upon a house that was so very, very small, I couldn't believe my eyes. I was intrigued. Such a tiny place, and standing all on its own looking lonely and isolated in this great wilderness.

Deciding that a photograph was needed, I grabbed Robert's Kodak Brownie and was aiming the camera and about to press the button, when suddenly there was a huge commotion. An old woman came rushing out of this little house and was shouting furiously at me from the garden gate. She clearly wasn't happy, and with anger like hers I feared for my life. There was no doubt about it – I had to run to safety. Speeding back to the car I leapt in without a backward glance, and Robert, amidst a plume of smoke, departed at speed.

Our encounter with the mad woman was only a small part of our week-long adventure, and it wasn't long enough, as all too soon we were back to work. Nevertheless, my first eighteen months at William Hollins had been quite enjoyable and without too much responsibility, it was an easygoing and carefree time. Not only that, I was still young enough to get away with certain activities to make my days more interesting – like flirting with the boys.

Furthermore, with Dad's intervention, my typing lessons meant I was one step closer to realising my ambition of becoming a secretary. In the interim I was more than happy to accept the offer of becoming a Dictaphone typist in the typing pool. This move not only gave me a pay increase, but it was also a job I enjoyed, as I loved doing everything at great speed.

My fearsome supervisor: Miss Cox, sat at the back of the office surveying her team of typists, and I could feel her steely eyes upon my back as she watched intently to see if I made any mistakes. Typists had to be extremely accurate, as any errors were all too obvious, with a special rubber being used to erase mistakes. And if not done neatly, the whole page had to be re-typed, together with two or three carbon copies, which also had to be corrected.

The typing pool was responsible for producing most of the letters and invoices throughout the company, but it was rather like working in a typing factory, as the desks were in rows and faced a blank wall. Then for those few snatched moments of daydreaming, the office had windows stretching the length of the room, offering a good view over the canal and city beyond. And Ann, who sat at the back of the office next to the window, became our weather monitor. Frequently declaring, 'It's a bit black over Bill's mothers.'

Miss Cox believed she had the best department within the company, as her standards were high, with all correspondence randomly checked to ensure there were no errors. She was proud of her girls and for that reason ensured we were given a good annual bonus – but we had to earn it. Punctuality, doing a good day's work and not having time off helped achieve our reward, although I was grateful for any extra, however small.

I was fast and accurate and became proficient at typing the weekly schedules; with my pride at an all-time high after typing thirty foolscap pages of figures without a single mistake. Thereafter, they were printed on the Gestetner printing machine, although using the Banda machine was less messy than ink and stencils.

After a while, I became almost totally responsible for the work that came through this small printing section. The benefits, apart from not sitting at a desk all day, included visiting other offices throughout the company. Along with my promotion, came the opportunity to visit Roger and Peter in the sales office. Despite knowing I didn't stand a chance, as they were way above my station in life, I continued to daydream of the possibilities.

Problems at Home

I loved my work, but problems were beginning to arise at home, and when I arrived with smudged mascara one day, it was obvious that I had been crying. I'd had a furious row with Dad the previous evening, and he'd threatened to throw me out on the street. It was only because I didn't know who else to talk to that I confided in two of the older ladies in the office. Joyce was about thirty years old, but as I was only sixteen and a bit, to me that meant she was really quite ancient. There was also Ann, who was a lovely motherly figure. They tried very hard to comfort me and help with my dilemma.

Whilst growing up we had been taught to sort our own problems out, so I kept all my innermost thoughts and feelings buried within my soul, trying to reason them out as best I could so as not to bother or burden anyone else. I don't think Angela had these problems, as she had plenty of friends, particularly Rita, who also became a friend of mine.

Before Father re-married and whilst we were in our early teens Angela, Rita and I became good pals and started going out together at weekends. At the time I was not old enough to go into a public house, let alone go on a pub-crawl. Nevertheless, that didn't stop me, as every week for many months, the three of us travelled around Nottingham on the bus. Our Saturday night entertainment involved visiting the many public houses in the region. In the mining areas, especially, the pubs were heaving with intoxicated people and the air was so thick with cigarette smoke – we could barely see across the room. Consequently, upon arriving home, my clothes smelt of cigarette smoke – and I had to wash my dress quickly before Dad became aware that we had been smoking too.

Despite our unladylike behaviour, Rita, Angela and I continued to drink in excess for the duration of our Saturday nights out. Then we crept in late at night, so as not to awaken Dad, as we didn't want him to find out what we had really been up to, as we knew he would be disappointed and quite shocked. There were occasions, however, when we found him lurking next to the front door as we very, very, quietly slipped the key into the lock.

Even though we had many good times, I remember little of this period in my life, but sometimes the memories of youth fleetingly flash through our minds, making sure we don't forget such moments. After a while we all went our separate ways, as people often do, seeking other interests and friendships. The chapters of life took the three of us in different directions, and in pursuit of our hopes and dreams and desires for the future. But we never forget special friends, even when they are from another part of our life.

Following this chapter in my life, and also, for the duration of my teenage years, I continued to look for someone special to enter my world. Like many young people, I suffered heartache and rejection from boyfriends. It's supposed to be part of the growing-up process, but the sorrow didn't do me any good.

Then a surprise: regardless of having a chaotic relationship with my father, out of the blue he suggested that he could afford to send me to the Clarke's school for hairdressing. It was a new venture and a modern concept in teaching these skills, and because he knew this is what I really wanted to do when I left school, I believe it to be the reason that he was making the offer.

In spite of this suggestion, I was sixteen going on seventeen and had become settled in my work, and anyway, I thought it was too late for me to learn new skills. After all, the majority of workers stayed in the same job for the duration of their working life, and I envisaged this was how my life would be too.

But it wasn't only that. My problems at home had become so overwhelming the idea of changing my job, and also, getting to know new people, sent me in a spin, and I turned Dad down.

Then my troubles and conflicts at home escalated to such an extent, that Dad threatened that I would have to find somewhere else to live if I didn't behave in a more appropriate and respectful manner. That, however, is easier said than done when you are a belligerent teenager, as despite trying to be nicer and more amenable, nothing seemed to go to plan and things just weren't working work out.

Chapter Twelve – Only Sixteen

Eventually it got to the stage where Father couldn't cope with me, and whilst still only sixteen I was asked to leave home. Even though I knew my behaviour was causing me such misery, I didn't seem to have control over my life. Feeling bewildered and unhappy, I was wondering what on earth I should do now. Then Angela, who was my best friend as well as being my older sister, came to the rescue. She was earning a lot more money than me and suggested we should get a bedsitter together.

Dad didn't literally throw me out of the door, but I knew I had to act quickly before that might happen, and, because it seemed sensible to find a place en-route to work, Sherwood seemed like a good idea. But with limited finances, a bed-sitter was all we could afford. Nonetheless, it was exceedingly small, with just one room and a kitchenette, and we had to share the bathroom at the end of the house with other tenants.

Life was difficult for us in the early months, as we were still very young and not experienced enough to fend for ourselves, let alone set loose into the world. Furthermore, money was a major problem and despite occasional pay rises, I was still earning a pittance and definitely not enough to pay my way. When times were really hard, we had to live on baked beans on toast until pay day at the end of the week. To make sure I didn't sponge off Angela, she often hid her spare cash and then forgot where she put it, as occasionally when tidying up, we came across money in the most unlikely of places.

We had both done cookery since early childhood and were capable of preparing a nice meal. Even so, this couldn't be anything too complicated, as our kitchen was just a cubbyhole with a tiny sink, a tiny cooker and a few pots and pans we had managed to scrounge from home. So we improvised and made the best of what we'd got.

My biggest problem came when I ran out of money by the middle of the week, so instead of a nice relaxing ride home on the bus after work, I walked. Wearing high-heeled stilettos was bad enough, but getting lost in dense swirling fog - which was a common occurrence in the 1960s, was a terrifying ordeal. Especially on an occasion when I could barely see my feet, and with a wall of fog surrounding me, I ended up walking the wrong way.

Bad weather wasn't our only problem. After a while our bedsitter was proving much too small, and with an empty room next to ours, we speculated as to whether the landlord would allow us to have it. However, being two shy teenage girls and without any spare cash, plucking up the courage to negotiate wouldn't have been so bad if we'd been able understand his foreign accent.

Friday, was rent night and our nerves had jangled all day, and got even worse as we waited for the landlord's knock on the door. By good fortune, he was in a jovial mood that night, and with the whiff of alcohol being all too evident; he'd clearly had more than a few pints. We were one up already! And the rest wasn't too difficult, as he was happy for us to paint and furnish the room at our own expense. Well, what a surprise!

This surely was cause for celebration, but first of all we needed to get Dad on our side. He'd had loads of experience as a handyman, and we could turn to him for advice. Perhaps, there was an element of guilt at having thrown me out, as he came round the following week with paint, brushes and a large pile of newspapers. However, it was a very large room and we needed some help, and that meant involving those who used our place to hang out when they fell out with their parents.

With a few flagons of cider on offer, there was no difficulty in bribing potential decorators, and in no time the painting was finished. At which point, Angela, being a whiz on the sewing machine, worked her usual magic by making curtains for the large windows overlooking the front road.

My Special Friends

Joyce and Ann, my two older friends from work, continued to show concern for my welfare. And as a consequence, Ann decided a kitten might heal the wounds of having to leave home. Her cat had had kittens, and she wanted me to have one too. It seemed like a good idea, as I hadn't forgotten Suki, my cat on the farm who went missing, so I decided my new kitten would also be called Suki. Angela wasn't happy with this new addition, as we could barely afford to feed ourselves, let alone a kitten. But I was desperate for someone to love and decided Suki would fulfil that need.

Initially, she had the run of our flat whilst we were at work, but after a while it became obvious it wasn't good for a small cat to be cooped up inside, and alone, all day. So a decision was made: she had to go outside in the morning. With a small back garden, she could hide under a bush or lie out in the sunshine until we arrived back home.

But warm sunny days weren't always on the horizon, and then it was horrid for a kitten to be outside when it was raining and cold. As a result, the lady in the flat downstairs often felt sorry for Suki and took her in, comforting her and feeding her when she was hungry. Ann thought she was doing me a favour by giving me a kitten, but it was quite the opposite: a pet wasn't a cure for my problems and simply made my life difficult and more complicated.

Before too long, it became apparent that I was being selfish in my desire for Suki to fill the place of someone to love. My long hours at work meant I didn't give her the time and love she needed, and my continuing financial crisis was causing an even bigger problem. Consequently, I decided that she needed a better life than the one I was offering, and someone else to love and care for her.

Then after a heartbreaking journey to the RSPCA, it was with immense sadness that I left her with them. My little Suki will forever be in my heart, but the feelings of guilt that I let her down and should have loved and looked after her better, still remain. But even without the pet food costs, my money worries were a continuing saga, my life had become impossible as I tried to make ends meet on a daily basis.

What's more, having swopped rock-and-roll dancing for posh parties, our social life had become more expensive, too. Attending these events without the latest trendy gear was unthinkable. I had no choice. I needed to earn more money to survive, and the only way was to take on extra work, which meant finding a Saturday job. There was no difficulty in finding work as there was a huge selection. But I wanted something to fit in with my employment at

William Hollins, as having worked there for several years it was an environment in which I felt comfortable, and also, about the only thing in my life that was stable.

Whilst searching through the vacancies in the *Nottingham Evening Post*, I was spoilt for choice, but decided a job at Stead and Simpson's shoe shop on Long Row would, if nothing else, give me access to discounted shoes. In reality, it was to become my saviour.

In fact, I made as much money working on a Saturday as I did working Monday to Friday with my office job. There again, it was also a time when working in a shop wasn't held in high regard, so I told very few friends and acquaintances of this other life of mine.

Before the new store opened, there was a major training day for the team of Saturday girls. The motto: 'The customer is always right' meant we had to accept whatever demanding shoppers threw at us. On the other hand, it wasn't only difficult people that were a problem, because after a while, I came to realise that by working six days a week I was missing out on my teenage years, with little time to enjoy this special period of my life. In spite of this, at the close of day I was rather smug with my earnings – at least I could survive another week without too much pain and misery.

Come six o'clock, I was desperate not to be serving a customer, as my mind was focused on dashing to the bus stop in order to get home as quickly as possible. Whereupon, a nice cup of tea and a comfy chair was all I needed. But as a seventeen-year-old, it wasn't the done thing to be home alone on a Saturday night. Particularly, as Angela had been hard at work lining up the best parties. Generally, her Saturday's were fairly leisurely. Following a quick flick round our flat with a duster, she embarked on a ten-minute bus journey that took her to Father's house. Visiting our new baby brother had become her favourite pastime, and, having a delicious home-cooked lunch in return for an afternoon of babysitting, I reckoned, was a great deal more pleasant than my busy day at the shoe shop.

I suppose I was envious of my sister, believing she had a prime position in life and a better existence than me. Perhaps it was because of my childhood experiences that I wasn't trusting of others and felt unable to share my troubles and worries with anyone else.

Supposedly, I had a 'chip on my shoulder', but they were just words, as I didn't really know what it meant until later in life.

Not only that, working six days a week and with little time to enjoy myself, I was fed-up with my dull and mundane existence, and upon waking early one morning, decided a window shopping trip would brighten my day. So I skived off work! All the same, I felt guilty, as skiving wasn't the done thing.

Following a leisurely lie-in, I took a short bus journey into Nottingham and alighted in the Old Market Square. Normally I only passed through the city early in the morning or late in the afternoon on my way to and from work, but to find it nearly deserted was quite a surprise. With almost full employment, shopping was usually done on a Saturday, with the husband and children in tow.

Then all of a sudden I had the jitters. What would happen if I was spotted by someone from work? Well that's not going to happen, I thought. Then as I was swooning over a lovely dress in the window at Griffin and Spalding, to my horror, I saw a colleague heading my way. To avoid detection, I needed to act quickly. If I hid behind one of the lions in front of the Council House, she would never see me. So I scurried from shop to shop before darting across the road, but too late, I was spotted as I peered from behind the masterful beast. Except he wasn't my protector; he had given my game away.

Reporting for work next day, I made my excuses to Miss Cox, but judging from her cynical smile it was obvious she didn't believe my story and would almost certainly get her own back on me come bonus time.

A Holiday in Jersey
Angela and I hadn't had a holiday since our trip to the Isle of Skye, so it was decided a trip to Jersey with a friend might be a good idea. This wasn't something I could afford, but somehow I managed to rustle up the money. But definitely not from my father, as he never loaned us money, making us stand on our own two feet was a discipline he never abandoned.

This was to be my first trip on an aeroplane, and I wanted to ensure I didn't stand out from all the other well-dressed passengers, as travelling in a casual or slovenly manner wasn't the done thing.

115

Once again, Angela came to my rescue. Being in need of something nice to travel in, she made me a beautiful suit. It was bright orange; a colour for the young and vivacious. With its lovely A-line skirt and box-style jacket, and worn with a navy-blue frilled blouse, it looked stunning. To make sure I didn't forget this beautiful outfit, a photograph was taken on the arm of a Swiss lad I met on the first day of our holiday.

For our flight to Jersey we travelled to Gatwick, which meant a long train journey to the airport. Maybe there were alternatives, but we probably wanted to show off to friends, as flying from a large airport was more impressive. To complement my new outfit, I bought a hat and insisted on wearing it for the whole journey, which was a bit daft really, particularly, as we were travelling in the middle of the night. Also, having bought enormous sunglasses – which were the latest craze, I wore those too. I reckoned they made me look important – and maybe, someone might mistake me for a famous person. Well, why not!

Overall, we had a fabulous time swimming and sunbathing – this being an important factor, as it guaranteed returning to work with a fabulous suntan; to prove we had been somewhere impressive. At the time holidays abroad were not the norm. A week or two in Skegness or Blackpool was more usual for most families and probably in a caravan or tent. But we wanted everyone to know that we had been for a posh holiday.

Upon arriving at our hotel, a new experience was awaiting us, by way of sharing a table in the hotel dining room with lads from Newcastle-upon-Tyne. They called themselves 'Geordies.' Not only that, they had a language of their own. Consequently, having a conversation with them was quite a challenge, as not being able to understand their dialect; it was like talking to a foreigner.

In spite of this, we only had to put up with them twice a day, as when the sun went down, moonlit evenings took over, and they were of the dancing and drinking variety. And with plenty of other young holidaymakers around, we had a jolly good time.

But two weeks wasn't long enough, and all too soon we were heading for home, but not before promising Norbert, my special beau that we would continue to communicate. He'd seen me walk through the door when arriving at the hotel and within hours he'd asked me out on a date, and because he was the assistant hotel manager and spoke nine languages, I thought he was incredible.

Once back home and realising our holiday was over for another year, depression set in. Having discovered a new way of life in Jersey, we were eager to return, and with a plentiful supply of jobs for girls like us, we would do whatever was required – chambermaid, barmaid, cleaner... the list was endless.

Meanwhile, we were anxious to do some partying and show off our suntan before it had a chance to fade into oblivion. Then after a while we settled back into our mundane life and our holiday became a distant memory. Daydreams lingered, but they faded away too. That's because the next best thing came along: a new boyfriend. But will he be forever?

St Ives

A year later Angela and I had another holiday, in fact it was with my father and Janet, my new step-mother; having lived away from home for a while, I was getting on with them much better. So much so, that Dad suggested we accompany them on a caravan holiday in Cornwall. Our little brother was about three years of age, and we knew there was a hidden agenda – we were to be used as babysitters whilst they went off ballroom dancing every evening.

However, with the suggestion of sun, sea and sand, it didn't take too much persuasion, although no mention was made that we would be setting off at three o'clock in the morning. Normally, the only time I saw that time of day was when arriving home after a night of partying.

Nevertheless, to ensure we couldn't hold up Dad's planned departure time he insisted we stay with him the night before, but at least we could sleep for the duration of the ten hour journey; even if it was a bit of a squeeze in his little Ford Anglia car. And with the prospect of two whole week's holiday, it was worth putting up with Dad's erratic driving as he lovingly gazed over the fields, instead of the road, as we approached Cornwall.

Along the way, Angela and I had decided that we needed to find out where other young holidaymakers hung out, and it was upon our first visit to the beach that we met up with a crowd of surfing fanatics. There were also many artists amongst this hippie's paradise, one of whom invited Angela and me back to his studio.

Stepping through the door I could see that he was certainly prolific, as every wall was taken up with a painting. But when he said 'I would like to paint your portrait,' I was flabbergasted. Feeling very flattered, I told my father 'Oh that would be nice' he replied. Except, little did Dad know I would be in a state of undress. Well, I might have had a liking for the lads, but I was much too bashful to expose my body to a stranger, so I turned him down. Besides, there wasn't enough room on his walls for another painting.

Whilst away, MaryAnn had moved from Stroud to work at the Queen Elizabeth Hospital in Birmingham, and with a short train journey to Nottingham, she was able to visit us more often. It also gave Angela and me the opportunity to take her shopping, even if this could be an exhausting experience. With MaryAnn being accustomed to marching up and down the hospital wards, she was able to walk much faster than we could run, let alone walk. Her flat shoes speeding along the pavements made it difficult for us to keep up, especially in our high-heeled stilettos.

There was also the matter of our Saturday night entertainment. If MaryAnn was to come out with us, then a plan of action was required. We insisted upon styling her hair and putting her make-up on, and making sure she wore the appropriate clothing. Being a nurse, she didn't normally bother with such things. Her hair was shoved under a cap and jewellery, make-up and nail polish wasn't allowed on the wards. But by the time we'd finished with her transformation, she was worthy of a night out on the town.

We enjoyed MaryAnn's visits, but my teenage years weren't always light-hearted and fun. All too often, I was fighting a losing battle trying to keep up with other girls of my generation. Many of them lived with their parents and had more cash to spend on clothes and girly things, whereas my money was going on rent and electricity bills.

Chapter Thirteen – The Party Scene

As time progressed, Angela and I became fussy about boyfriends, and because we didn't have transport of our own, we insisted they had a car, and preferably, a sports car. The Black Boy Hotel in Long Row was usually our starting point. From here we found out where the best parties were likely to be and bagged a lift from someone desirable. Downstairs was always heaving with young people, swigging gin and tonics and talking very posh, but upstairs, where the older and more sophisticated couples hung out, was even posher.

Then with transport lined up the length of Long Row, we were ready for the off. But which car was it to be? The Lotus Elite was the best, but we were happy with an MGA, or even a Triumph TR4, but preferably not an MG Midget, as it usually came in last. Top of my list was an Austin Healey 3000, which, with the roof down took seven with a squeeze. Hanging out from all corners was terrific fun and such a thrill as we raced around winding, narrow country roads, and going much too fast.

However, things didn't always go according to plan, like when Angela managed to get a lift with Peter, a smart young man with an E-Type Jaguar. I'd never managed to catch the eye of this particular beau, and would have done anything to have been in her shoes that night. To make things worse, my lift to the party was somewhat different, as I was pushed into a Mini Cooper. Not that there was anything wrong with the Mini, as it was the latest trend in cars - but it wasn't an E-Type Jaguar.

Even worse, the driver of the Mini was so busy chasing the Jaguar that it went round the corner too fast and ended up in a ditch. The outcome was some excruciatingly painful fractured ribs, which put me out of action for a while. Well, not too long really. After all, I wasn't going to let a few cracked ribs get in the way of my social life.

Despite my suffering, several weeks later I ventured back into the party scene and all was going swimmingly, until some great hunk of a man picked Angela and me up together and gave us a big squeeze. The experience was agonizing and required more than a gin and tonic to get me through the night.

Two Weddings and a Cathedral

I was not quite eighteen when MaryAnn married, and naturally Angela and I were bridesmaids. Angela used her expertise to make our pretty lemon-coloured dresses, and with lots of petticoats to make the skirt stand out, they were perfect for teenagers, like us.

Robert's special day came a year or so later and was somewhat different from his twin sister's wedding. In view of the fact that he and his betrothed were studying at Brackenhurst College, they were in the catchment area to marry at Southwell Minster. Angela and I were thrilled, as we knew this was going to be a special dressed up occasion for us girls.

Once again, Angela excelled in the making of our bridesmaids' dresses. With fitted bodices and long skirts and made in pale turquoise silk taffeta, they looked stunning. Walking down the aisle, I could hear the rustle of my skirt and see the material glistening like little silver droplets; and I felt this was my special day too. After the service, and thinking I might be next in line to find myself a man, I leapt into the air to catch the bride's bouquet. But rather disappointingly, someone else got there before me.

Some years later I tried to alter my dress into something more appropriate to wear for other occasions, but it didn't work out as intended and ended its life being shoved into the back of the wardrobe. Now, all I have is a photograph to remind me of how young and beautiful we looked: my sister and me.

Tormented Teens

Over the turbulent years that followed, I was desperately seeking love and happiness. Frequently, I daydreamed about how wonderful it would be when I met my special man. On the contrary, most lads weren't interested in love and friendship – they wanted something else, and it wasn't just a kiss and a cuddle. And as for the sweet nothings in the ear! I was misguided into thinking they were words of love. Vulnerable and gullible, I believed everything I was told.

In the fullness of time, I discovered that their smooth talk and ardour was in fact meaningless and all they wanted was a one-night stand. Despite having lived in the city for several years, basically I was a country girl at heart, and extremely naïve. I had also been brought up never to tell lies; only little white lies were permissible. Because of this, I thought everyone else had the same standards and values, but found this not to be so.

But there was also someone special in my life – Johnny. He was different from other lads and extremely handsome. With his dark hair and sultry looks, he looked like Elvis Presley. How could I fail to be smitten? We went out together for some considerable time, even though I have to admit to the odd fling in-between, which was partly because our relationship was more or less on a part-time basis, as he often worked away.

When he was back at weekends we had lots of fun, but come Monday morning, fed-up with being parted, he wanted me to share his life in Manchester. It was an attractive proposition, but worrying about leaving Angela alone in our flat, I turned him down. How different my life might have been had I taken up his offer.

For three years in succession Johnny and I visited Cornwall over the Whitsun holidays. Despite still working at the shoe shop, as I had done every Saturday for several years, he persuaded me to have a weekend away with him. Nevertheless, I was concerned at the prospect of taking time off, particularly, as losing money would cause me a major problem. Eventually, temptation got between me and having a good time, so I skived off work.

We left on Friday evening and travelled through the night to make sure we got ahead of the crowd. All the same, great care was needed, as the West Country roads could be treacherous, with few dual carriageways to overtake the inevitable slowcoach. Johnny had also kitted his Mini Traveller out so that we could have a short rest if tiredness, or even, if a moment of passion got in the way of our journey. But at least our night-time driving ensured we had the best place on the beach, and, the best place to watch the rising sun.

Setting up camp was quick and easy too, as Johnny had purchased the latest inflatable igloo tent; a new innovation and much better than the traditional type. But in view of the fact that we only had a few days to make the most of the sun, sea and sand, and to take home a glorious suntanned body, we needed to sunbathe from dawn till dusk. To achieve this, we got a head-start by using olive oil for the purpose of tanning as quickly as possible. Unfortunately, it had the opposite effect on me, as I burned and turned bright red.

I was suffering badly one day, when a wise old local lady approached me on the beach and, realising I was in need of help, suggested the best way to ease my pain and suffering was to bathe in milk. Bathe in milk! I thanked her for her words of wisdom, but declared, as we were camping, that was easier said than done.

In spite of this, I managed to survive my ordeal and at the end of our short holiday, life quickly returned to normal. Johnny went back to Manchester and I returned to Nottingham. And not very popular either, as upon returning to the shoe shop I was on the receiving end of stern warnings from my boss. Which I took with a pinch of salt, as I believed it would only be a matter of months before I could pack up in my own good time.

Some months after our third trip to Cornwall Johnny announced his decision to explore the world, but said, 'I will come back for you and then we will travel the world together.' Before departing, I gave him a photograph to remind him to come back home to me.

I'd never been anywhere, apart from Jersey and the Isle of Skye, and was thrilled at the prospect of such an adventure. To make sure that I was ready for the journey of a lifetime, I started collecting all the things I might need. Then I put my life on hold and waited for Johnny's return. That did not happen. Had he found a new love? I never found out.

Despondency set in as the months came and went, and still no contact from Johnny. Then Angela, aware of my melancholy, suggested that as we'd lived in Sherwood for several years, we should look for a change of scenery and with a friend wanting to share with us, we would be able to go upmarket. West Bridgford being our first choice. So we scanned the local newspaper for a suitable place, but without access to a car, our only method of transport was the bus. Even so, having passed a garage on Arkwright Street and noticing that petrol was four shillings a gallon, I realised I would never be able to afford to run a car, let alone buy one. In the 1960s, it was mostly only girls who were well-off and privileged, with a car of their own.

So our search for a flat began. With plenty of choice, but taking into account the proximity of the bus stop, we settled for a place on Mabel Grove. The flat above had been taken by male students from the university, whilst Angela, our friend Anne and I, had the ground floor.

Anne immediately commandeered the large room at the front of the house; being like a bed-sitter it gave her the option to entertain friends without interference. She reckoned that as Angela and I were sisters we wouldn't mind sharing the smaller bedroom. Though I rather suspect, it may also have been because of a skin disorder, as there were occasions when we assisted in applying ointment to the affected parts, after which, she had to be wrapped in polythene bags; hilarious for all, but the recipient.

Next to our bedroom was the sitting-cum-dining room, which led into a kitchen that was almost as grim as our cubbyhole kitchen in Sherwood - but much colder, to the extent that in winter we lit the gas cooker to give a glimmer of heat. What's more, the loo was outside and not nice when paying a visit in the middle of the night. Through the back door and round the corner, our smallest room was cold, damp, dark and had plenty of creepy-crawlies. Needless to say, it wasn't the right place to sit and read one's favourite magazine.

Once it had been an elegant home; the high ceilings and ornate cornices made it feel special, but on the other hand, it was difficult to heat. For this reason we purchased coal from the local merchant; with ten pounds' worth giving us enough fuel to last through winter. Arriving a few days after placing an order, the fuel was tipped directly down the chute into the cellar below.

At the time, the coal merchant was a regular sight on the roads, as most houses had a fireplace and a chimney. There was a price to be paid for this method of heating though, as every morning without fail the fire had to be cleaned out; the ashes were then put into a bucket outside the back door. Nothing went to waste, as with the arrival of spring, the ashes were dug into the garden by the enthusiastic landlord to help his veggies grow. But we didn't do things like that as we had better things to do than grow lettuce and beans.

Our New Flatmates

Having moved in about the same time as the three lads upstairs, it was decided we should have a housewarming party. For Angela and me it was our first since my sixteenth, but not wanting a recurrence of those problems, this party was carefully planned. Nevertheless, with such a diverse selection of friends, invitation was by word of mouth. And that is probably where we went wrong, as by the time the party was in full swing, it became apparent there were many unfamiliar faces. Where did they all come from? We didn't have an answer.

Loud music and drunken behaviour quickly took over, with the place heaving with young bodies in all four corners of every room. Then in the early hours of the morning, things got out of hand and the long arm of the law descended upon us to sort things out.

Whilst in the process of organizing the party I got to know one of the guys from upstairs, and he became my dancing partner for the evening. He was a likeable person and the sort of boyfriend my father would have approved of. So why didn't the friendship develop beyond the first few dates? Perhaps, it had something to do with his putrid, turquoise-coloured car, which was a mile from a sports car and definitely not the latest trend. On the other hand, this poor hard-working student couldn't afford a smart car and rather unkindly, I preferred to be seen in something trendier than an Austin A40.

The father of another of the lads was a director at the Mars chocolate factory and after every trip home, he returned loaded with chocolate bars. These handouts were lifesavers, as I used them for the times when I was too hard-up to buy a sandwich for lunch. Many times his Mars bars made the difference between catching the bus and having to walk home after work.

Our friendship with the lads continued for the duration of their studies at the university, and because of this we often shared a Sunday roast. They bought the meat and we provided the veggies and labour to cook this traditional Sunday meal, and with pudding for afters, it was good enough to see me through the week.

Eventually, the lads moved on and shortly afterwards Anne left too. We'd had many good times and it was a sad moment when we went our different ways. And now, with only Angela and me, we went in search of a smaller place. Then another of our friends decided she wanted to leave home and share a flat with us. So we scoured the adverts in the local newspaper until we came upon a possibility. But three storeys up? That surely could be a problem if we happened to arrive home a bit tipsy after an evening out. All the same, it was big enough for three, and the best we could get for our weekly budget of five pounds.

In a previous life the attic rooms had probably been used by servants, as the tiny windows in the sitting-cum-bedroom made it dismal and dreary, which probably disguised the fact that it hadn't seen a lick of paint for many years. Not to be put off, Angela and I, who had become accomplished decorators, brightened the place up in no time at all. Apart from the fact that we'd clearly scrounged the paint from Dad, as the kitchen and bathroom, in their entirety, were covered in ice blue paint – which wasn't exactly the right colour to make it appear cosy and warm.

Nevertheless, everything else was perfect, except for the electricity coin meter, which seemed to be out of control – gobbling our hard-earned cash with amazing regularity. So we had to do something about it before we ran out of money, and it was suggested we try the age-old trick of a coin on a piece of string. Supposedly, if a coin was inserted into the slot and then swiftly pulled out again, it triggered the mechanism, and hey presto – free electricity! No such luck for us. We had to revert to our tried and tested method of bribing whoever was willing to put money in the meter.

Not only did we attempt to control the electricity meter, but in the back garden was an archaic wash-house where, to try and make ends meet, I washed a suit that should have been dry-cleaned. I had bought the outfit after seeing an attractive girl at the Vale Hotel in Daybrook. Her gorgeous white suit, blonde hair and flawless suntan had the men vying for her attention, and I decided that I wanted to replicate her style.

125

And it was at my favourite shop: C & A Modes that I found what I was looking for. The beautiful white jacket and slim-line skirt was unlike anything I'd had before. Believing this sexy little number was bound to attract the lads, I handed over my hard earned cash.

Nevertheless, the lovely soft woollen material must have got in the way of my senses, blinding me to the fact that it would never stay that way. To my detriment, I found that after wearing it a few times grubby marks appeared as if from nowhere. What was I going to do now? I washed it! But only because I was unable to afford dry cleaning bills. When I pulled it from the water I cried in disbelief, as I knew instantly it had shrunk beyond redemption. With no way of going back in time and unable to afford to replace my lovely outfit, I shed more than a few tears that night.

That wasn't my only problem; a bigger setback was about to hit Angela and me. Our friend, who was in the process of moving into our flat, had changed her mind. She offered no explanation, but it was a massive blow. How could I possibly afford to pay my way?

With greater outgoings I decided there was no option, other than to find another job. Having worked at William Hollins for four years and more, and from the day of my fifteenth birthday, I was reluctant to leave. Not only did I feel secure with my surroundings, but in my turbulent world it was my sanctuary; working alongside people I'd grown to trust and doing a job I loved.

There was no difficulty in finding employment, as there was a plentiful supply in the office world, and I was more than happy when offered a job at the Zurich Insurance company in the Old Market Square. However, the work was vastly different from my previous job, with lots of jargon and gobbledegook. Even worse, the girls were clique and unfriendly.

Consequently, it didn't take long to realise I needed to move on, and by good fortune, when visiting the Trent Bridge Inn one Friday night, I met a guy who was looking for a receptionist-cum-secretary. Someone who was willing to make the tea and do whatever was required. He was a director in his electrical company and offering an excellent salary. Convinced it was fate that this chance meeting had come about; I was in no position to turn him down.

The downside: the office was much further away from West Bridgford and a jolly long walk home when I ran out of money; which I seemed to do with great regularity, and for this reason, I was in no position to give up my Saturday job.

Even though I was jolly pleased to have found this new job, I had come to realise that I was so busy working and making ends meet, that my teenage years were slipping away, denying me the leisure time that many of my generation took for granted.

Despite my financial situation, it didn't stop me from going out, as we had a set pattern for our weekend entertainment, starting with Friday and jazz night at the Trent Bridge Inn. Whilst some of our friends went upstairs to become inebriated, we headed for the dance floor, with Pete as my favourite dancing partner.

Then one Friday night Pete and I, amongst others, were dancing in front of a television crew who were filming youth of our generation. Fortunately, I was wearing my new emerald green skirt and French-navy blouse; a combination that I had bought from Jessops department store on the never-never. This eye-catching outfit was similar to one I had seen Kim Novak wear – she was a famous film star whom I adored, and whenever possible, I tried emulating her style. Pete and I were dancing partners for several years, during which time I grew fond of him. Then he went to London to become a shoe shop manager, so yet again, another chapter of my life came to an abrupt end.

At least our move to Musters Road was timed right, as there were many jazz clubs in the area and they had become the latest craze. With The Dancing Slipper in West Bridgford, on our door-step and being well known for big names, such as Acker Bilk, Kenny Ball and Chris Barber, we were fortunate to see these great musicians. But it wasn't only the jazz bands; we also loved to dance, the Stomp being the way of dancing to traditional jazz. Also, because we wore casual and comfortable clothes, we sat on the floor in-between dancing without fear of getting dusty or creased up. Such an easy-going atmosphere made it a great Saturday night out.

Chapter Fourteen - Skegness in the Middle of the Night

But as time went by my life had become a round of work, parties and drinking too much, which in all probability was to deaden the pain. A glimmer of fun in-between the mundane kept me going. I liked flash cars, high standards and perfection, but I was still searching for something else – even though I didn't know what it was. After the rock-and-roll era, my biggest crisis had been when I was asked to leave home. No matter what I did thereafter, I never seemed able to overcome my financial difficulties

And now, with many of our friends pairing up for life, the party scene was diminishing too, as Angela and I and two friends found out one Saturday night. We had been on the rounds looking for a good party, but it was one of those times when nothing was happening. Well, we could go to the Kardomah coffee house, or perhaps an Indian meal? Or even a Chinese? There was also, the newly opened all-night ten-pin bowling alley. But none of these appealed. With a beautiful starlit night, why not a trip to Skegness to stroll along the beach under the moonlight?

Never having been to Skegness before, let alone in the middle of the night, it seemed like a good idea. So past midnight we jumped into Jim's car and drove in an easterly direction. Most folk were tucked up in bed, so we had the road to ourselves, and with the car roof down we watched the stars as we sped through the night. Arriving in Skegness as dawn broke and with the sun peeping over the horizon, we realised there was to be no moonlight stroll for us.

What were we to do now? And it was whilst driving along the sea front that we found the answer. Sand dunes! They were perfect for a snooze and some peace and quiet. Not only that, we could remain undetected from prying eyes, as the sea breeze massaged our aching bodies and the sound of the waves calmed our senses. We didn't need to count sheep either, as we had big white fluffy clouds, even though they were in a great hurry as they raced across the lovely blue skies.

After a short kip and determined to make the most of our time in Skegness, we decided upon a paddle in the sea. Much bravery was needed for this so called pleasure, as when dipping my toe into the water, being so very cold, I swiftly pulled it out again. Well, perhaps a stroll along the promenade? But even that was quite a battle, as our flimsy dresses were no match for the bracing easterly winds; whisking them high above our knees and flirting with our petticoats.

If nothing else, the sea breeze left us feeling re-energised and ready for our onward journey. Once back home, the nearest we got to water was the Victoria Embankment alongside the River Trent; with fairs and festivals taking place throughout the year, it was a popular place for young and old, alike.

Other interests included motorcar racing at Mallory Park and Silverstone. This activity was probably enjoyed more by the lads, as many of them had sports cars and were great racing enthusiasts. After the race and their ambitions of becoming a racing driver in full throttle, they used the same tactics as Stirling Moss on narrow country roads. Consequently, our drive home was rarely conventional, and often, more like a ride in the wild.

A more sedate weekend activity was watching the water skiing at Hoveringham. Despite not being a water lover, it was a good enough reason for a trip into the countryside and afterwards, a visit to the Ferry Boat Inn. Many of the young congregated there for a few pints, before driving home unhindered and without any possibility of a chance meeting with a man in a blue uniform.

Over the years, we had lots of good times - partying being one of our many pleasure. But most of all I loved the barbecues and outdoor events. Being part of the flower power generation – a time of freedom and liberation – dancing under the moonlight on a balmy summer's evening with a handsome young man, was just the best.

Turmoil and Confusion
On the other hand, was I merely trying to escape the realities of life, as for much of the time I still felt surrounded by turmoil and uncertainty, as I lurched from day-to-day, surviving week-to-week and in no position to plan my future. Money was a constant worry, or rather the lack of it; stopping me from making decisions about my

life ahead. Then Angela found herself a new boyfriend, and my world changed forever. Apart from being good friends, over the years I had become to rely on her; she made my dresses and bailed me out when I was hard-up. But now everything was going to be different. Until, quite unexpectedly, Johnny returned. I was thrilled! He hadn't forgotten me after all. Except after only one night of passion, he was gone again. I never saw him again, and it was many years before I was able to cast him from my mind.

Suffering rejection and probably on the rebound, I met someone else. Standing at the bar in the TBI and wearing a brand-new suit, he looked very handsome, and similar to my idol, Steve McQueen. 'Would you like a drink?' he asked. And when he invited me out on a date, there was no way I could refuse, particularly, as I had no idea when I might see Johnny again.

After this first date we went out together for some time, but on an irregular basis, as he had other leisure pursuits. A keen motorcycle enthusiast, he travelled to various rallies and races at the weekend. Even if I had wanted to, I was unable to get involved with this side of his life, as I worked every Saturday. In the past, Angela had ridden on a motorbike, but I was too much of a coward, so I guess it was unsurprising that I didn't show an interest in this activity.

Then some months later I had a dreadful shock, and a very unwelcome surprise: when I discovered there was going to be a new life entering into the world. Yet again, I had another problem to sort out on my own.

Despite my age and even though I had grown up on a farm, I was extremely naïve about the facts of life. Being of such a delicate nature, these things were never discussed while I was growing up. And at no time throughout my adolescence did I have anyone to talk to. I knew there was a risk of pregnancy by becoming too intimate with a lad, but I had no idea how that came about, so I continued to hope for the best.

Following this discovery, I went into shock and subsequently disappeared from the social scene for several months. Then by the time I came to terms with my predicament, my Steve McQueen lookalike had a new woman, so there was no going back in time.

It was a terrible crisis to face, and all alone, as I didn't have anyone to confide in, not even my family, as I was too ashamed and embarrassed to admit to my plight. This was a shameful situation and the reason many young women went to special mother and baby homes who dealt with 'girls in my position.'

They were sent away and out of sight of neighbours, friends and even family, until it was all over. Following the birth of their baby, they would be allowed back into the family fold once more, nobody knowing the truth behind the weeks and months they had been absent from home.

There were no options, apart from backstreet abortionists, so like many young girls; I had no choice, other than to go through with the birth. The state wasn't a provider for unmarried mothers and for those who were unable to take their baby home to live with their parents, the child had to be offered for adoption.

Whilst growing up, we had been taught to sort our own problems out, but as I didn't know how to resolve this problem, I tried to ignore my quandary and get on with life – until the time came when I had to face up to reality.

Not having been to see a doctor for years, I nervously went to the local surgery. It was a time when I was seeking help and reassurance, but instead, the male doctor was horribly unpleasant, as he had no patience for girls like me. With such a stigma attached, I was treated like an underclass. So I went to see another doctor, but he didn't come up with a solution to help with my predicament, either.

It was a terrifying ordeal. At night I walked the streets in a daze. Round and round, up and down the same roads, trying to puzzle out what I should do next. Then Angela decided to move to a new life in London with her boyfriend, and immediately, I knew what I had to do. This would give me the opportunity to move to another area and disappear off the planet for a while.

After moving out of our flat at Musters Road, I stayed at my father's house for a few weeks, and even though I should have said something, I was too scared of the shame and disgrace it would bring to the family. So I remained silent, in the hope that I could work something out in my own time.

More Problems

Looking through *The Lady* magazine, I found a family requiring a home-help in a large house in Barnes, south-west of London. It was the first job I applied for, and when offered, I accepted the position readily, as I felt there would be few opportunities for girls such as me, who required sanctuary and work for a few months.

All the same, it was a dreadful way to treat a young girl away from home, as things started to go wrong almost immediately. My tiny bedroom was at the top of the three-storey house, and being painted in a mushy pea-green colour, made me feel that I was in the servant's quarters. I cried constantly, as I was utterly miserable in my new surroundings, and still I hadn't told my family, or indeed anyone else, why I had moved so far away from home.

But at least the sunny skies offered a little respite and allowed me to daydream. Often whilst hanging the washing out for the matriarch, I watched the aeroplanes flying in the skies overhead. There were so many, crisscrossing and flying in all directions; and as I stood watching, I was so wishing I could be up there and flying off to some magical place. Somewhere, anywhere, other than the place I was in right now. I made a promise to myself that when this was all over, I would fly off to some wondrous place - wherever that might be, I would explore the world and have a wonderful time.

The lady of the house knew of my troubles, but also took advantage and gave me some pretty horrid jobs to do – although she had a beautiful mahogany dining-room table which I polished with great enthusiasm. There again, I'd had many years of practice during my childhood, and it was one of those tasks I most enjoyed; and she reckoned, I was the very best at this particular job.

Eventually, when I could no longer put up with living and working in my environment, I confided in MaryAnn, my eldest sister, who said she would help me out. Her husband was working away, and it was a huge relief when she offered to let me stay at her place for a while. She had been a nursery nurse, and was now a mother herself and had plenty of experience of motherhood.

Without hesitation, I packed the large trunk that I'd purchased before my move to Barnes. Stored inside were all my worldly possessions, and also, a little furry rabbit and tiny baby clothes that I bought on my days off. I hid them away, all those special things that I didn't want to share with anyone else.

It was such a bitter-sweet experience, I was elated at the prospect of getting out of this terrible place, but at the same time, I felt daunted by what lay ahead. Would it be the best or the worst time in my life? Even though my employer begged me to stay for a few weeks longer until she had found a replacement, I couldn't go through another day of this torment. Without delay, I arranged for my belongings to be collected and sent down south, and it was a joyous moment when I caught the next train out of London.

The weeks ahead with my sister were comforting. She was experienced in the ways of the world, not judgmental, and wanted to help out with my predicament. So I had a carefree and relaxed existence for a while. Being summer and living close to the sea, we often went to the beach; a nice casual stroll, with no rushing or hurrying and very different from the hurly-burly of the city.

I didn't have to worry about money and making ends meet, or shopping for food, and all the other problems that had been part of my life for so many years. I didn't even need to think ahead, as I had already decided that a new home would be found when this new little being eventually came into the world.

Then early one Sunday morning my baby boy arrived. Fortunately, it was a quick birth, as I had been left to suffer all alone, with no one to hold my hand or help me out. In spite of this, the love I felt for this new baby overrode the suffering I had been through over the past months.

And that is when my troubles really began, as prior to my son's birth I had already made a decision to have him adopted, but now my plans had suddenly disappeared into oblivion. A mother's love is very powerful and strong, and with my own mother having died whilst I was under the age of three, and with two step-mother's following in her footsteps, my endless search for love had finally arrived.

After the birth I was placed in a ward with three other young mums, but whilst they had a visit from their baby's father every evening, I buried my head under the blankets and sobbed uncontrollable. In different circumstances, the cottage hospital would have been a wonderful place for the two weeks recuperation; even withstanding being woken at five in the morning with a mug of hot sweet tea.

Tears of joy, but also dreadful sorrow, streamed down my face as I cradled my beautiful baby, whilst the doctor stood by and showed no signs of sympathy as he said 'You should give him up for adoption'. He could say that of course, because to him, I was just another silly girl who'd got in to trouble, but without any visible signs, he wasn't to know that my heart was breaking.

Ignoring all warnings by those who thought they knew better, one thing was for certain, I wasn't going to give my baby to anyone else. Consequently, an uncertain future lay ahead for me and my son, and I had to do something about it. But before such time, a name was required – so I called him Martin.

To start with I needed to let my father know, particularly, as I'd just had my twenty-first birthday and I knew that he had been planning to celebrate. So I wrote a long letter explaining exactly what had kept me away from home for so long. Perhaps he was angry and annoyed with me – after all, this would discredit the family name, but he didn't show it. Instead, he was sympathetic and suggested I return to Nottingham. With nothing to stand in my way I headed back north with my precious cargo.

My little brother had just started school and I helped out by collecting him every afternoon. I also assisted with jobs around the house, which gave me plenty of time to perfect my skills at becoming a mother. Furthermore, I welcomed the fact that I had time to reflect on my position in life, as everything had changed.

Becoming a mother had made me a different person and I had to think carefully about what lay ahead. And regardless of being happy living in my father's house, it wasn't like a real-life situation and I sought more. Besides, I wanted to share this perfect baby with someone else, as my biggest sorrow was that two parents and not one should have been around at such a magical time.

Then whilst looking through the local newspaper I came across an advert by a gentleman wanting a housekeeper. It sounded perfect, so not wasting any time I followed it up, and was pleasantly surprised to find that the position was in a peaceful hamlet in north Nottinghamshire, and exactly what I was looking for.

In spite of my situation it was important to get things right, as I had a lifetime ahead and great consideration was needed for me and my little boy. I consulted with my father, but he wouldn't get involved, saying, 'You are an adult now and must make your own decisions in life.'

After the events of the past year, there was no way that I was looking for, nor indeed, interested in a relationship. My aim was solely to have a settled existence in a pleasant environment where I could raise my son. Anxious to find this new life, I telephoned the number to discuss the position and was immediately smitten by the beguiling voice on the end of the line.

Upon meeting Jack - the owner of that voice, not only was I overwhelmed by his stunning house, but also, by his hypnotic charm. Almost immediately, I knew there was little chance of finding such an opportunity again, and without hesitation, I rushed home to start packing as I didn't want anyone else to step in before me.

Dad was a little taken aback by my hasty actions, but I'd made my decision and there was not stopping me now. The large trunk that had seen me through some difficult times whilst I was living in Barnes was just the right size for mine and Martin's worldly possessions, and they were transported to our new home.

The first few weeks started off reasonably well, even if living in a house with a stranger proved to be somewhat different to when Angela and I had shared a house with other people. But those good times were short lived. And I was left wondering what I'd let myself in for. However, with few options for an unmarried mother, and with nowhere else to go, I had to get on with it. Also, having moved from my father's house in such a speedy manner, I didn't want to admit defeat by asking to return.

But how naïve I must have been to believe that happiness was mine for the taking, as without realising it, within a short space of time Jack had taken control.

Neither did I know that he had crossed my path before, not once, but twice. Whilst I was growing up in the Cotswolds, he was flying his little RAF trainer aeroplane over our house. Then again, a few years later, having moved to Nottingham with my father and sister, he was living with his parents a mere half mile or so from our house.

And so it turned out, over the coming months and then years, Jack took my life over. How could I possibly have known that I would have to be incredibly brave with this new encounter? Life was certainly going to change, but not in the way that I had wanted, or even expected. I'd had to cope with many problems throughout life, but such trials and tribulations would stand me in good stead for the years ahead. Helping me to be strong and able to survive some of the bad times coming my way. Even though I'd been through a lot of change and turmoil whilst growing up and, as a teenager, they were nothing compared to what was in store for me.

This man, who was about to enter into my life was incredibly pleasant and charming – to me and to all other women too. I soon discovered that he was a compulsive womanizer; it was an addiction that he couldn't control. Over the next thirteen years he stole from me what should have been some of my best years. Whilst he spent his life having a good time, he took my happiness and replaced it with destruction. The heartache was so powerful that I couldn't forget, and trying to survive the ordeal took all my energy away. Finally, when my son and I broke free of this man and his torment, I vowed to put pen to paper. But that is a story for another day….

THE END

WHO'S WHO

Mr Great-Grandparents

Arthur James & Annie Sherriff

My paternal Grandparents

Wilfred Fowler & Mary Ellen Sherriff

My maternal Grandparents

Arthur & Minnie Cross

My Parents

John Dumella & Dorothy Ann Sherriff (**Mother**)

My Siblings: Robert, MaryAnn & Angela

Pamela –my 1st step-mother (**Mum**)

My sisters – Sophia and Louise

Janet – my 2nd step-mother

6818409R00084

Printed in Germany
by Amazon Distribution
GmbH, Leipzig